ADDED
TO THE
CHURCH

ADDED
TO THE
CHURCH

A
CHURCH OF GOD
MEMBERSHIP
MANUAL

BILL GEORGE

Pathway
P·R·E·S·S
CLEVELAND, TENNESSEE 37311

ISBN: 0-87148-031-X

LOC: 87-061050

DEDICATION

This book is dedicated

to my sons,

Michael and David

F O R E W O R D

King David said, "I was glad when they said unto me, let us go into the house of the Lord" (Psalm 122:1). True disciples today also love the house of the Lord and the congregation of believers.

Service to the Lord in the community and throughout the world flows from local congregations. Therefore, it is vital for believers to come together and be equipped to serve. This book fits into the discipling process in which local congregations equip members to better fulfil their God-given calling to service.

The idea for this book emerged from a brainstorming session of the Church Training Course (CTC) program committee. Bill George was a member of that committee. During the discussion, he shared his burden to write a book of this type. The response of the committee and the General Board of Youth and Christian Education was very positive and his dream was greeted with excitement. A pastor on the General Board said, "We have been waiting for a book like this for a long time." He verbalized what many pastors across the denomination have said many times before.

As General Director of Youth and Christian Education I am pleased to have *Added to the Church—A Church of God Membership Manual* as a part of the CTC program. I know it will be welcomed by all Church of God members today, and it will be used to equip new members for many years to come.

To God be the glory as His saints are discipled and equipped for service.

W. A. DAVIS
General Director

P R E F A C E

The vitality of any movement arises from its sense of identity. We in the Church of God must know who we are and what we believe in order to carry out the mission the Lord of the Church has given us.

A person has a right to understand fully the tenets of those whom he or she is joining, and the church has a scriptural responsibility to ensure that its members believe in the biblical and theological principles it espouses. Unfortunately the church has not always been diligent in this responsibility. Too many churches operate according to the rule, "If we can just get them to become members, they will eventually accept our theology and practices." This is an obvious violation of a person's rights and the church's responsibility.

In this book Bill George presents a clear treatise for those who want to know what it means to be a member of the Church of God. From his rich background of theological studies and pastoral experience, he shares what it means to be a part of the body of Christ and demonstrates why membership in the Church of God is a meaningful spiritual experience.

This book is long overdue. It should be required reading for all Church of God members, regardless of the length of our membership, for it reminds us of truths we may be in danger of forgetting. It definitely *must* be read by anyone who is contemplating membership with the Church of God.

As you examine *Added to the Church* in the perspective of your own personal experiences, I pray God will help you take seriously the biblical mandate to be the salt of the earth and the light of the world. May being part of the Church of God help you to become all that God has in mind for you to be. Hundreds of thousands of brothers and sisters around the world are ready to support you.

R. LAMAR VEST
Assistant General Overseer

TABLE OF CONTENTS

The Church Training Course Series

Added to the Church by Bill George has been designated in the Church Training Course Program as CTC 321. The certificate of credit (CTC 321c) will be awarded on the basis of the following requirements.

1. The written review and instructions for preparing the review are listed on page 95. The written review must be completed and evaluated by the pastor or someone he designates. Then the name of the student must be sent to the state office. (No grade will be given for the written review.)
2. The book must be read through.
3. Training sessions must be attended unless permission for absence is granted by the instructor.
4. The written review is not an examination. It is an overview of the text and is designed to reinforce the study. Students should search the text for the proper answers.
5. If no classes are conducted in this course of study, Church Training Course credit may be secured by home study.

A training record should be kept in the local church for each person who studies this and other courses in the Church Training Course program. A record form (CTC 33) will be furnished upon request from the state office.

Added to the Church

I grew up in church from my childhood, probably taking church for granted as many people do. Early memories of church are pleasant for me. I remember a boys' Sunday school class where I usually sat leaning back against the wall in a wooden chair tilted on its back legs until the teacher told me to sit up straight and listen. I recall a Vacation Bible School where we fashioned wall decoration plaques from small, paper-thin copper plates. One of the most vivid recollections is the Easter Sunday when I was eleven, walking down a church aisle to tell the pastor I wanted to give my life to Jesus Christ. Church was always a warm, amiable place for me.

When I was a teenager our family moved. The new church was large and I did not immediately find a niche. Although I attended more or less regularly, I was not involved. Soon afterwards I met a group of young people who were members of the Church of God. They were excited about their church and they could not tell me enough about it. One of them gave me a little tract, "Facts About the Church of God," which contained basic information about the denomination and a listing of its beliefs, along with Scripture references. Since some of the doctrines seemed pointedly different from what I had learned, I began reading the verses and making notes about them. Long discussions followed over school lunches and after school.

One evening I accepted an invitation to accompany some of my friends to a special meeting. Their church was sponsoring a tent revival in another part of the city in an attempt to start a new congregation. We arrived late at the crowded tent. That night, in the first Pentecostal service I had ever attended, I responded to the evangelist's call to receive the baptism of the Holy Spirit and experienced a personal Pentecost. It was a life-altering moment.

The next day the pastor of the Church of God talked to me about becoming a member. My head was swirling with questions. To make a long story short, however, I joined the church a few weeks later.

I have often wished that the pastor could have placed in my hands something that would have answered my queries. To be sure, the subsequent teaching I received from the pulpit, Sunday school classes and young peoples' meetings, together with my own personal reading and study, eventually satisfied my desire for information about the church. Friends with whom I have shared my experience have told me that they, too, have wished for a membership manual which would supply basic facts about the church.

Added to the Church is written for people who want to know what it means to be a member of the Church of God. It attempts to answer several basic questions: What is the church for? How does our particular church, the Church of God (Cleveland, Tennessee), relate to the scores of other Christian churches? How did our church begin and how has it grown? How is it organized? What essentially are our doctrinal beliefs? How may I be a faithful, productive, spiritually maturing member of my church?

One of our continuing concerns in the Church of God is that our beliefs and practices always mirror the example set for us in Scripture. The first principle accepted by the church remains at the heart of its existence: The

New Testament is our rule of faith and practice. With this orientation, it is instructive for us to begin our examination of the church by looking at the Book of Acts, which chronicles some of the events of the earliest years of the church. The goals, concerns and accomplishments of the young church become the model for our own.

The earliest description of the church in action may be read in Acts 2:41-47, which details the experiences of the post-Pentecost fellowship. The record states the following:

41 Then they that gladly received his word were baptized: and the same day there were added unto them about three thousand souls.

42 And they continued stedfastly in the apostles' doctrine and fellowship, and in breaking of bread, and in prayers.

43 And fear came upon every soul: and many wonders and signs were done by the apostles.

44 And all that believed were together, and had all things common;

45 And sold their possessions and goods, and parted them to all men, as every man had need.

46 And they, continuing daily with one accord in the temple, and breaking bread from house to house, did eat their meat with gladness and singleness of heart,

47 Praising God, and having favour with all the people. And the Lord added to the church daily such as should be saved.

What characteristics marked our model church?

They were committed to and responsive to the Word. When the Word of God was proclaimed by the man of God, it produced an active response. Peter's Pentecost Day sermon, which takes up most of Acts 2, was replete with biblical (Old Testament) content. Glimpses at other sermons preserved in Acts let us know that the Word of God and the acts of God in Christ formed the basis of preaching content. One mark of a New Testament Church is its faithfulness to the Bible.

They obeyed. The converts submitted themselves to water baptism, which had been commanded by Christ. This act of obedience signaled a mindset that patterns subjection to the law of Christ for His modern-day followers.

They celebrated results. On the Day of Pentecost, 3,000 of Peter's hearers accepted the gospel. The comment at the end of the passage (verse 47) indicates that the Lord kept on adding to the church on a daily basis. God's church today expects regular growth in numbers of people.

They demonstrated consistency. "Continued stedfastly" carries with it the idea of perseverance and discipline.

They evidenced concern with proper belief. While the writer of Acts does not go into detail about the content of their doctrinal study, he labels it "the apostles' doctrine," which we can interpret as the teaching or example that Christ had communicated to His disciples, which they, in turn, shared with their followers. Based on the later content of their preaching and writing preserved in the New Testament, we can accurately reconstruct it. It included a high view of the Old Testament as God-originated, information about the life and deeds of Christ, together with His ethical and practical teaching.

They enjoyed fellowship. The Acts picture of the church shows them in frequent company with one another. They worshiped together in the Temple, ate together in homes, prayed together, observed the Lord's Supper together and spent time together as friends. Their togetherness obviously went beyond the formal union that takes place in a worship assembly; they actually delighted in being with one another.

They prayed. The pattern of the Master had not been lost on them. They seemed to realize that Jesus

Christ had done what He did as a result of His prayer life, and they emulated His example. Prayer kept them in active communion with the Lord of the church.

They practiced caring stewardship. This earliest portrait of the church reveals people whose mutual love was so great it inspired them to go to sacrificial lengths to actively care for one another. They sensed personal responsibility for each other. None of them was content to have too much if another had too little. This precedent exemplifies the concern that today's church should demonstrate for those in need.

They witnessed miracles. In the early church the believers accepted the word of Jesus, "He that believeth in me, the works that I do shall he do also; and greater works than these shall he do; for I go unto my Father" (John 14:12). As a result, signs and wonders took place. These attracted public attention and authenticated the Christians' message. Today's church is still heir to God's promises to heal and deliver. A church that is faithful to the New Testament example will evidence faith in God's ability and willingness to do what men say is impossible.

They were liked by the people. If a first-century resident of Jerusalem wished to know what it meant to be one of God's people, prior to the advent of the Christian church, his model would have had to be a member of one of the Jewish religious parties. He might have observed a worldly Saducee or a legalistic Pharisee, but their witness would have transmitted an undesirable image. How different was the testimony of the Christians! Their ebullient joy, contagious enthusiasm, warm caring and reverent disposition was winsome indeed. As a result, people liked them and were attracted to them. God wants that kind of church today!

The description of the Jerusalem church establishes an ideal that the Church of God strives always to reach. We believe that our fidelity to Christ may well be marked by how we measure up to the standard set for us by the apostolic example.

The research for this book has caused me to lay aside a cherished notion that I held at one time: That the Church of God is the same everywhere. If that were ever true, it is not true today. In a spiritual sense, of course, the church enjoys unity. As far as the biblically based fundamentals of the faith are concerned, we do not and cannot differ. In the words of the hymn, "We are not divided, All one body we, One in hope and doctrine, One in charity."

But I have discovered variegated beauty in the local expressions of the denomination. In a certain city, for example, one congregation prefers singing time-honored hymns and contemporary choruses, while another church likes gospel songs and convention songbooks. I have observed that some Church of God people feel comfortable in small congregations and others would rather attend large churches. One pastor preaches only expository sermons, while his neighboring pastor's messages are almost always topical in nature. The constituency of one church is largely professional and middle-class, while across town another church's membership is mostly mill workers with lower incomes. Not far away is another church whose members live on farms. Of course, each of these churches probably includes a few people who differ somewhat from the majority, but all are good general descriptions of the kind of dissimilarities that occur.

These differences alarm some people, but they may be one of our best signs of good health. Church history and our own denominational history teach us that churches which become culture-bound wither and die. One of the earliest crises through which the apostolic church passed was the Acts 15 controversy about the Jewishness of the church. Certain leaders were requiring new non-Jewish converts to accept Hebrew cultural and religious practices before they could be full-fledged Christians. The leadership of the young church considered the matter and, guided by the Holy Spirit, voted a resounding "no" to the requirement. The church must always guard against cultural encroachments into its doctrinal province. We cannot allow our culture or the traditions of men to influence us away from the norms of Scripture. It is a mark of effectiveness, however, when a denomination can penetrate differing cultures and present the unchanging gospel in such a way as to attract faithful followers of the Lord Jesus Christ.

The fact that our church differs in small ways from congregation to congregation has made this a difficult book to write. Which church do you write it for? Every Church of God preacher who has observed our variety will sympathize with me in the task. I have tried to address the broad middle ground of the church as I perceive it. I understand fully that not every pastor or lay member will agree with every statement and observation in the book. I ask, however, that it be accepted as a beginning point for Church of God membership orientation and that whatever additions or alterations are necessary will be offered with an appropriate scriptural explanation.

"The Lord added to the church . . ." is the Bible's way of affirming that it is, indeed, *His* church. While we do not lay claim to be God's only people by any means, we believe we stand on firm scriptural ground in defending our faith. My hope and prayer is that *Added to the Church* will help its readers be the best members they can possibly be.

Bill George

They That Gladly Received

*I*n the United States, some 330 different Christian denominations exist, including 45 Baptist groups and 12 Catholic movements besides the Roman Catholic Church. Handbooks that list North American religious organizations show more than 40 churches in which the words "Church of God" appear.

This book is about the Church of God (Cleveland, Tennessee). The town and state where the church's international offices are located—Cleveland, Tennessee—are written in parentheses in legal documents after the biblical nominative "Church of God" to distinguish this body from groups with similar names headquartered in other places.

Where does the Church of God fit with all the other Christian churches? How is it similar to them? How is it different? This chapter will answer these questions and will explore the New Testament idea of what the church is and ought to be.

THE CHURCH OF GOD IN PERSPECTIVE

Before Jesus Christ ascended into heaven, He made provision for the work which He had begun on earth to be carried on after His departure. He established the church, gave instructions about its purpose, and later sent the Holy Spirit to empower it. From this standpoint, we may say that the church is a divine institution. It was divinely planned, established and commissioned.

The word *church* came into the English language from the Greek *kuriakon*, which means "belonging to the Lord." The New Testament, however, uses a different word for church, *ecclesia*, which literally means "the called out ones."

The earliest pictures of the church are the ones described in the Book of Acts and the epistles of the New Testament. These writings portray local bodies of believers functioning in their communities, cities and regions, proclaiming the gospel and nurturing new converts; and cooperating in inter-congregational enterprises to care for the needy and to spread the gospel to places where it was unknown. Delegates from the churches gathered in a central place when the need arose to discuss matters of faith and practice, and the congregations on a local level accepted and implemented the decisions of the gathered body of leaders.

Growing political strength in the city of Rome, together with the presence of ambitious leaders at the head of the congregations there, brought the church in the capital city of the Roman Empire into early prominence and into eventual control of the other churches. From about A.D. 500, the church that became known as the Roman Catholic Church dominated Christianity, although history records frequent and numerous dissenting groups.

For about a thousand years, the situation remained much the same until the Reformation movement, initiated by Martin Luther in Germany, brought into being a succession of national churches unattached to the ' Roman Catholic Church. From the time of the Reformation in the 1500s until the present, the development of the Christian church can be likened to a tree whose limbs have grown in all directions—some large and some small, some straight and some twisted, some bearing fruit and others fruitless.

The Protestant Reformation brought into prominence again the truth that the only definitive source of spiritual authority is the Bible, the Word of God. The way the Bible should be interpreted, however, has been the subject of much disagreement through the years. The result is that many different denominations have been established.

Churches today may be categorized in many ways: by their theological positions, their national origins, their governmental polities, their doctrinal peculiarities or other distinctives. The following paragraphs attempt to relate the Church of God to its sister communions in the Christian family.

Catholic or Protestant. The Roman Catholic Church, headed by the pope in Rome and operated throughout the world by a hierarchy of cardinals, archbishops, bishops and priests, bases its beliefs on the Bible and church tradition. The Orthodox churches (Greek, Russian, and so on) trace their roots to the Roman church; but they divided from Rome because of doctrinal and political controversies in the early middle ages. Most other Christian churches are called "Protestant" because they protested the beliefs and practices of the Roman Catholic Church. The Church of God is classified as a Protestant church.

Liberal or evangelical. Liberalism, sometimes called "modernism," is a general term used to identify movements popular within some branches of the church in the last two hundred years that have tended to weaken or deny faith in the authority of Scripture and remove the element of the supernatural from the Christian religion. Evangelicalism, on the other hand, affirms basic doctrines as revealed in Scripture, such as the Trinity, the deity of Christ, full inspiration of the Bible, the death of Christ as atonement for sin and the second coming of Christ. The Church of God is an evangelical church.

Pentecostal or charismatic. In a sense we may think of these designations as interchangeable, since both refer to manifestations of the Holy Spirit. In common parlance, however, *Pentecostal* usually refers to the family of denominations that began around the turn of the twentieth century, churches whose worship patterns and doctrinal faith are like those described in the Acts 2 account of the events on the Day of Pentecost. *Charismatic* is commonly used to identify churches with similar practices which began more recently. Many Pentecostal denominations were strongly influenced by the holiness movement of the late 1800s, which emphasized the biblical idea of separation from the world. Charismatic congregations have often arisen from disparate backgrounds; some stress the holiness aspect of Christian life and others do not. The Church of God is a holiness Pentecostal church. Other Pentecostal churches that bear some similarities to ours are the Assembly of God, Pentecostal Holiness, Foursquare Gospel and Church of God in Christ.

National or international. Probably no Christian church of any denomination answers to the true ideal of a universal church. The Church of God began as a United States church with a foreign missions program. Over the years the number of members in countries outside the United States has grown to exceed the number within the country. Since the early days of its missionary activites, the church has sent not only American missionaries, but also ministers from other countries as its emissaries and ministers. As the church has matured, its leadership has begun to call for an increasingly international church. Men of other countries have been elected to membership on its highest governing councils. The church is moving toward becoming an international church.

THE NEW TESTAMENT IDEA OF CHURCH

The Church of God, which traces its beginnings to an Appalachian mountain community prayer meeting in the 1880s, has sought to rediscover and implement in today's setting the New Testament ideal of Christ for His church. The men and women who founded the church and shaped it were themselves products of various religious heritages, including Baptist, Methodist and Quaker. Ecclesiologists who look for influences of these denominations may find them, but the church's early leaders earnestly believed they were directed by the Holy Spirit in discerning beliefs and practices from the Bible.

A well-known theologian and ecumenical spokesman wrote a landmark magazine article in the early 1950s in which he called the Pentecostal movement "the third force in Christendom" (after the Roman Catholic Church and traditional Protestant churches). He made the startling observation that if the Apostle Paul were to visit today's world, he would probably feel more at home in a congregation like the Church of God than in any other kind of church.

What does a New Testament church look like and act like? The following paragraphs attempt to capture the essence of the biblical description and the reality of today's Church of God. The statements in italics represent our understanding of what the church ought to be, but we acknowledge that every local congregation may not possess every single characteristic of the ideal church.

The Bible is believed and acknowledged as authoritative. Our church has proclaimed definitively and forcefully its absolute trust in the inspiration and authority of the Holy Bible. The first statement of our Declaration of Faith affirms, "We believe in the verbal inspiration of the Bible." We understand that the Word of God comes as a revelation given by God Himself to man. It is infallible, final and complete.

Why such an insistence upon the authority of Scripture? If man does not have a source of truth above himself, he is left on his own to discover it. While science abundantly demonstrates that the pursuit of knowledge may be challenging and rewarding in the natural world, no parallel exists in the supernatural world. We learn only what God chooses to reveal. That revelation, we believe, is contained in the words of the Bible. We believe its writing and preservation were guided by the Holy Spirit. Science, individual conscience and human reason are valuable, but fallible; God's revelation alone is fully trustworthy.

Our defense of inspiration is threefold. First, Scripture itself teaches inspiration (2 Timothy 3:16, Galatians 1:11-12). Second, fulfilled prophecy confirms the truth of the Book (e.g., Luke 4:17, Luke 24:27, 2 Peter 1:19). Third, our own experience, along with that of Christians through the centuries, validates its claims.

In our kind of church, we are in constant danger from competing sources of authority. Emotionalism, individual personal experiences, so-called "words of the Lord," personality cults, pronouncements of men—all must be submitted to the authority of God's Word. It instructs, analyzes, evaluates and judges.

Nurturing and training are given attention. In the Book of Acts, which records the activities and ministries of the first century church, much importance is attached to training. Jesus, in His parting instructions, had emphasized the teaching function of the church (Matthew 28:19, 20). Verses such as Acts 4:2,18 and Acts 5:21, 25, 28, 42 affirm that the disciples took seriously His command.

The Church of God devotes much of its resources of people, time and energy to the ministries of teaching and training. A careful analysis of pastors' pulpit content usually reveals a strong teaching emphasis. An hour each Sunday morning is set aside for formal study of the Bible and its application to daily living. The midweek service in most local churches is called Family Training Hour. Additionally, the denomination plans periodic concentrated training programs to augment the weekly efforts. These include an annual week-long Church Training Course prepared by the General Department of Youth and Christian Education; a program called Bible Institute for Ministerial and Lay Enrichment sponsored by the Department of General Education; frequent training retreats and conferences offered by the Department of Evangelism and its Lay Affairs office; and an annual seminar on ministry scheduled by the School of Theology in Cleveland, among others. Further, the Church of God sponsors colleges in key geographic areas and a graduate-level theological school for ministerial training.

The content of our teaching is important. We stress doctrinal matters, edificatory sharing and practical training. We have discovered that this triple approach is necessary if believers are going to grow in the knowledge of the Lord Jesus Christ (2 Peter 3:18) and apply that understanding to their lives.

The end result of our teaching efforts is men and women who become more Christlike, full of the Spirit and divinely enabled to accept and fulfill spiritual ministries.

Evangelism is primary. We believe that the church legitimately may be involved in many ministries, but the highest priority should be assigned to soulwinning. Sin has separated individuals from God, and our primary calling is to mediate the saving gospel of Christ to the world in order to reunite them with Him. Abundant evidence exists in Scripture to undergird the primacy of evangelism; examples include 2 Corinthians 5:18-21, Ephesians 3:1-11, Philippians 2:9-16 and Colossians 1:18-29.

The Book of Acts describes the evangelistic efforts and successes of the church, which we take as a pattern. Chapters 8-12 are especially instructive, revealing that everyone connected with the church seemed to take evangelism seriously. It shows ordinary lay people testifying of their faith, a deacon conducting a city-wide evangelistic crusade and church officials directing the continuation of a revival meeting. The following chapters of Acts indicated that varied techniques were employed, including public proclamation, household visitation, one-to-one conversational approaches, the use of healing and miraculous signs and strategies designed to plant churches in pioneer areas. Evangelism was the heartbeat of the first-century church; we believe it should be the same in the twenty-first century.

A pastor/laity partnership insures successful ministry. The Church of God attempts to recover the balance, obscured or lost during many centuries, between pastoral leadership and lay ministry. Within a few generations of its founding, the Christian church had moved toward a system that placed responsibility for all ministry in the hands of professional clergymen, changing the role of church members from active participants to passive spectators. The Protestant Reformation gave lip service to the doctrine of the priesthood of all believers, but churches that came into being following the Reformation still depended essentially upon the pastor for all spiritual ministry.

In the Church of God we believe that the Bible ordains that called men of God should indeed furnish leadership to local churches (e.g., 1 Corinthians 4:17, 1 Thessalonians 3:2, Titus 1:5, 1 Peter 5:2), but that the men and women who make up the membership should also actively participate in ministry. Churches that depend solely on the pastor's efforts are unable to carry out the Lord's purpose for His church; and churches that are totally dominated by lay people have departed from the biblical pattern. Our church has consistently attempted to resist traditional ecclesiastical pressures which call for professional ministers to perform all spiritual service. At the same time, we have tried to be aware that our secular civil governmental system of democracy has nowhere been appointed by God as His method of directing the church. This is a new idea to individuals who come to us from churches where, because of political situations, lay-controlled structures have evolved which do not take seriously the biblical model of cooperation between God-called leaders and their followers (e.g., Acts 6:2-5).

Four New Testament passages in particular point up the relationships that ought to exist between pastor and members: John 10:2-4, 1 Thessalonians 5:12, 13, Hebrews 13:17 and 1 Peter 5:2, 3. These teach clearly that God calls certain individuals to serve as pastors or overseers of local groups of believers. These men are to receive God's direction, exercise leadership, provide spiritual care, labor with their people and give an account to God for them. Members, on the other hand, are enjoined to follow their pastors, recognize them and honor them. The church has made wise provision for dealing with unfortunate situations where inept or unfaithful pastors have come into leadership (this is treated in a later chapter of this book).

Ministry is accomplished on the basis of spiritual giftedness. One of the early affirmations of the Church of God, clearly out of step with the mainline churches of the time, was our belief in spiritual gifts. The New Testament gives a lot of attention to this truth, mentioning frequently the exercise of gifts. Important passages include Romans 12, 1 Corinthians 12, Ephesians 4 and 1 Peter 4.

We accept the biblical imagery of the church as the body of Christ. According to this figure, Christ is the head of the church (the Body) and each of us is a member, or part, of the Body. This means that just as every physical bodily part has a function, so each of us has a purpose to fulfill as a member of the Body. The eye's function is seeing, the nose's function is smelling. In the body of Christ, my primary purpose may be teaching; yours may be discerning of spirits or giving or exhorting; another's may be interpreting a message in tongues. Scripture lists many gifts which, working together, make it possible for the Body to function as God designed it to do. Christians ought to occupy their places in the Body based on the spiritual gifts with which the Lord has graced them. We know that it is God himself, by means of His Spirit, who apportions the gifts, and we acknowledge that He may follow any pattern which pleases Him with respect to the manifestation of gifts. We do not determine what our gifts are; He does. He may manifest His gifts in any manner, whether or not it suits our predetermined ideas or appears orthodox to us.

Fellowship is a normative aspect of the Christian faith. Church of God people greatly enjoy spending time with one another in informal settings. Recapturing the Book of Acts emphasis upon a two-tiered approach to meeting together—"in the temple and from house-to-house"—congregations in our denomination usually program activities apart from worship which allow personal interaction.

Christian fellowship meets a God-created human social need. Psalm 68:6 declares, "God setteth the solitary in families." Communion with brothers and sisters allows us to share and grow. Contrasting sharply with the practice of some sister denominations of imposing silence in the sanctuary before and after the worship service, the meeting places of our church are apt to resound with pleasant greetings, impromptu laughter and the happy chatter of conversation between friends. This glad warmth is not a mark of irreverence for the House of God; on the contrary, it is living proof of the Word of God which affirms, "Behold, how good and how pleasant it is for brethren to dwell together in unity!" (Psalm 133:1).

In our church we have learned that opportunities for fellowship are best realized in age-level groups such as Sunday school classes. Choirs, Men's Fellowship, Ladies Ministries circles and other special interest gatherings complement the fraternal activities. A few pastors in recent years who followed the brief trend of discontinuing the Sunday school quickly discovered that it had to be reinstituted or else replaced with something similar to provide fellowship occasions. We have observed that the new converts who are most likely to stick with the church are those who are quickly integrated into the church on the fellowship level. Since the ideal size for fellowship groups, according to reliable sociological studies, lies between 30 and 80 people (and sometimes may be stretched upward to perhaps 120), we have learned that our churches tend to level off at around a hundred and stagnate unless we create new classes or groups within the framework of the church, which can accept and integrate newcomers.

Healing by the power of God takes place. It was not strange or unusual in the experience of the model church of the New Testament for healing and miracles to occur. Jesus Christ had powerfully demonstrated His loving and efficacious concern for suffering humanity; in His name the young church acted to bring the same deliverance to the hurting men and women with whom they came in contact. It seems that every miracle was a sign which conveyed messages of faith to believers and conviction to unbelievers.

The Church of God still proclaims, along with the message "Jesus saves," our conviction that Jesus also heals. In most congregations prayer is offered for the sick who ask for it, according to the formula of James 5:14-16, with the faithful expectation that God can and will divinely intervene to bring relief from suffering and a return to health. The record of divine history reveals that the Sovereign God has at certain times demonstrated His miraculous power in greater measure or in more concentrated manifestations than at other times. The Old Testament exodus of the Hebrews from Egypt was one such time; the tandem ministry of Elijah and Elisha was another. The third concentrated period of miracles was the first century when signs authenticated the ministry of Christ and augmented the initiation of the infant church. In our own day, with the appearance of the latter-day outpouring of the Holy Spirit (Joel 2:23), we are witnesses again of an unusual display of God's wonder-working power. It would be difficult to find a local church in our movement without individuals who testify to having experienced acts of divine healing, some of them notable healings.

The Holy Spirit is experientially present. The Apostle Paul instructs us that God wants the church to be the place where the Holy Spirit lives and operates (Ephesians 2:20-22). Since in the thinking of God the church is not a building but people, we understand that God's desire is for the Spirit to indwell us as individuals. We then respond to His influence within us and will to do His will. Just as the Old Testament temple of God was filled with God's presence on its day of dedication (1 Kings 8:1-11), the believers on the Day of Pentecost were filled with the Spirit of God (Acts 2:4).

The Books of Acts, in its journal of some of the happenings of the first thirty years of the church, mentions the Holy Spirit more than fifty times. Even when He is not mentioned directly, His presence is sensed. The Church of God today seeks the same relationship with the Spirit of God.

To us the Spirit is not an impersonal force or benevolent influence; He is a person. He guides the church only as He relates Himself to individual believers within the church. We are truly God's church when we expect and respond to His direction.

How may this be seen in actual practice? Men and women are empowered for witness and service, and they perform it; lost people respond to conviction of sin and cry out to be saved; healings occur; bound people are delivered; messages in tongues are given and interpreted; prophecies are uttered; sanctifying power transforms the lives of yielded individuals; faithful stewardship of possessions is demonstrated; fellowship and communion is enjoyed; and unity prevails. If any of these manifestations are missing, then we cannot claim that the New Testament pattern is being followed and we ought to seek the reasons why.

Prayer brings results. The New Testament church was a praying church and today's Church of God aims to emulate its first-century example.

The followers of Jesus had evidently been powerfully impressed with His prayer life. They observed Him taking lengthy periods of communion with God (e.g., Matthew 14:27, Luke 6:12). They heard Him offer brief prayers prior to performing notable miracles (John 6:11; 11:41, 42). They knew that He prayed in times of crisis (Luke 22:39-46). It is no wonder, then, that they did not ask Him for instructions about how to perform miracles or healings; rather, they requested that He teach them to pray. They later remembered what He had taught them, and they made prayer a major essential of church life. The record states, "They continued stedfastly . . . in prayers" (Acts 2:42).

The Book of Acts records eighteen answers to prayers prayed by the Christians, modeling for us prayers for healing, boldness, deliverance, strength, conversion and divine direction. Paul's written prayers in his epistles let us know that it is legitimate to pray for knowledge of God's will, for unity, for hope, for growth and maturity, and for other spiritual and material needs to be supplied.

Our local congregations believe in praying. It is common to hear worship leaders call for Christians to share their requests for prayer with their brothers and sisters. Although the logistics of larger churches have caused this practice to be constricted in some cases, most churches have groups where specific prayer needs can be voiced.

The Church of God is a praying church because we believe God will hear and answer the petitions of His children.

SUMMARY

The foregoing paragraphs have attempted to describe the church in action—the New Testament church and the Church of God in the world today.

Our church believes in an authoritative and inspired Bible; it gives attention to training; it makes evangelism primary; it seeks partnership between pastors and lay people; it recognizes God-given spiritual gifts; it enjoys fellowship; it teaches divine healing; it allows the Holy Spirit to move as He will; and it believes in prayer.

This is the church we see in the pages of Acts. It is the church we seek to be as we yield ourselves to God.

CHAPTER REVIEW

1. The _____ _____ brought into being a succession of national churches unattached to the Roman Catholic Church; the_____ _____

brought into prominence again the truth that the only definitive source of spiritual authority is the Word of God.

2. Churches today are categorized in many ways; name four of them.

3. Explain the difference between liberalism and evangelicalism.

4. Explain our threefold defense of inspiration of Scripture.

5. List four terms to classify the Church of God as it relates to its sister communions in the Christian family.

They Continued Stedfastly

*T*he Church of God forms part of the fountainhead of the Pentecostal Movement which began in the United States at the beginning of the twentieth century. A hundred years ago no Pentecostal organization—not even a single Pentecostal congregation—existed; but in our day church demographers count scores of Pentecostal denominations in countries around the world whose total constituency exceeds 50 million.

The global Pentecostal family of churches is larger than any other Protestant grouping, including Baptist, Methodist, Lutheran or Presbyterian.

Students of Pentecostal history observe that our churches should not be discerned narrowly as comprising a distinctly new movement; but rather as institutionalizing a revitalization movement of the Christian church. Even a quick glance at the many obvious similarities between the apostolic church of the first century and Pentecostal churches today reveals a close relationship. Some early Pentecostal preachers pointed up this fact in their sermons and writings.

This chapter seeks to recount a brief historical summary of the Church of God, beginning with a few remarks about the scope of church history in general. Important highlights in the development of the denomination will be mentioned, and key persons who have influenced the church will be identified. The definitive history of the church is Charles W. Conn's *Like a Mighty Army*, from which much information in this chapter is taken and to which readers who desire a detailed study are referred.

HISTORY AT A GLANCE

Our understanding of church history may be summed up briefly as follows: Christ willed the beginning of the church and brought it into existence on the Day of Pentecost with a fiery baptism of the Holy Spirit. The earliest members of the church were obedient to the commission of Christ—to make disciples and teach them God's truth—and the Christian movement quickly spread. Within three centuries of its founding, however, the church, which had become extensive and influential, bowed to the control of unspiritual leaders who led it gradually farther away from its original purposes and beliefs. A long period of spiritual darkness followed, with only brief glimmerings of faithfulness found essentially among groups labeled as dissenters and heretics by the mainstream powers of Christendom.

In the 1500s a reformation movement began under the impetus of a Roman Catholic monk named Martin Luther, manifesting itself ultimately in groups that broke away from the established church and formed separate churches and denominations, most of them along national lines. These churches reflected varying degrees of fidelity to the doctrines and practices of the New Testament model.

To certain individuals throughout history whose lives have been marked by piety and concern for spiritual things, a fresh vision has appeared of biblical precepts and their incorporation into personal and church life. History identifies various men and women of this sort; among the most significant was John Wesley, an eighteenth-century Englishman. Wesley and his colleagues inspired a revitalization movement from within the

Church of England. The crux of their spiritual rediscoveries was that Christians' lifestyles should be affected by what they believe. The power of God saves men and changes them, they taught. They wrote their theology into hymns and sang, "Be of sin the double cure, Save from wrath and make me pure." Their emphasis on sanctification and their subsequent rejection by the Anglican church caused the birth of the Methodist church. Shortly after its founding in England, the church established congregations in America.

Some observers of church history have noted what appears to be a cyclical effect in denominational development. A church is born with vigor, enthusiasm and commitment; moves through a period in which it becomes formally organized; arrives at a time of maximum effectiveness; then begins to stagnate in an organizational morass; and slowly and finally disintegrates. At some point far along in the process, a revival may stir the movement to fresh life or inspire the genesis of a new movement.

The ecclesiastical scene in the closing quarter of nineteenth-century America was circumscribed by congregations with little or no spiritual vitality. Many factors had combined to produce an atmosphere in which churches were generally passive and ineffectual in combatting sin. The scourge of the Civil War and its bitter reconstruction aftermath; the effects in the religious world of Darwinian evolution theories in the scientific realm; the influence of German liberal theologians who questioned the authority of the Bible; the rise of the Populist movement in politics, which emphasized the common man over against autocratic authority figures—all of these elements and others working together created a climate of insecurity, uncertainty and powerlessness in the church world.

Our view of sacred history, however, affirms that God has always had a people faithful to His name, believing in His Word and obedient to His leading. Such men and women were used of Him to raise up the Church of God.

DAWNING OF A MOVEMENT

A spectacular revival meeting led by a black preacher named William J. Seymour at the Azusa Street Mission in Los Angeles, California, in 1906 caught the attention of public newspapers and the religious press. Word of the reoccurrence of events similar to the Day of Pentecost (Acts 2), with individuals being filled with the Holy Spirit and speaking in tongues, spread like wildfire over the nation. Dozens of churches and associations of churches dotted over the country, made up of hungry-hearted people, heard the news of the twentieth-century Pentecost gladly, and received it with the expectation that it could be repeated in their own experience. Other churches rejected it.

The strategic location of the Azusa Street outpouring in a populous metropolitan area like Los Angeles guaranteed the wide publicity that followed the unusual phenomenon.

Ten years previously, however, in the backwoods fastness of the southern Appalachian Mountains where the borders of Tennessee and North Carolina meet, a similar event had preceded the well-publicized Azusa Street occurrence. In the Shearer schoolhouse in Cherokee County, North Carolina, a revival led by lay preachers was attended by small groups of Christians who normally gathered in small congregations on both sides of the state line. While they worshiped together in the mountain schoolhouse on that evening in 1896, the Holy Spirit fell on them as in the first-century Upper Room, and many began to speak in tongues.

The Shearer schoolhouse revival was a high point for Richard G. Spurling Jr. and his church members who took part in it. A decade earlier, Spurling and eight neighbors had responded to an invitation from his aged father, Richard G. Spurling Sr., a former Baptist preacher, to start a new church. The day of the founding was August 19, 1886, the date the Church of God recognizes as its official beginning. The place was a rural community in Monroe County, Tennessee.

The elder Spurling had died shortly after the church's inception, and his son had been pastor of the group since then. A friendship with another lay preacher named W. F. Bryant, who lived a few miles away in the adjoining county, had led to fellowship and cooperation in the revival where the Pentecostal phenomena occurred.

The Spurling father and son, Bryant, and the laymen who led the meeting were typical of godly people in the mountains and in various parts of the county who had become weary of the lack of spirituality in the existing denominations and longed to see churches with vibrant power. The birth of the Church of God did not happen in a vacuum. During the closing decades of the nine-teenth century and the beginning of the twentieth, some thirty different organizations with holiness and Pente-costal distinctives came into existence. The Church of God makes no claims to exclusivity—although zealous men who confessed our efforts to duplicate as exactly as possible the pattern of the New Testament church did make that pretension at an early time in our history.

The small group who started the church in 1886 had answered Spurling Sr.'s invitation: "As many Christians as are here present that are desirous to be free from all manmade creeds and traditions, and are willing to take the New Testament, or law of Christ, for your only rule of faith and practice; giving each other equal rights and privileges to read and interpret for yourselves as your conscience may dictate, and are willing to sit toge-ther as the Church of God to transact business as the same, come forward."

Four men and five women formed the charter member-ship. Although their leader had used the term "Church of God" in his proposal for membership, they initially called themselves by the designation "Christian Union." The name expressed their desire to attract people from the lifeless churches of their community and from the world who would join a fellowship of New Testament

Christianity. Their group did not grow much in the succeeding years until the 1896 outpouring of the Spirit.

DEVELOPING A DENOMINATION

The early leaders of the Church of God were lay preachers. They attended the church's pastoral needs when they were not working in fields, keeping shop or operating a mill. Apparently the first full-time minister, a man who profoundly affected the development of the infant denomination, was A. J. Tomlinson.

Tomlinson, a Quaker from Indiana, arrived in the mountains as a Bible salesman. Attracted by the sincere faith of the people of the Christian Union, he soon joined them and eventually became their leader. In the years following the 1896 Holy Spirit revival, the church had begun to expand, establishing new churches in nearby communities. When representatives from four local congregations came together for a meeting for worship and business in 1906, the articulate and capable Tomlinson moderated the proceedings. They called the first gathering, in Murphy, North Carolina, a General Assembly, based on a Scripture reference in Hebrews 12:23.

During the years preceding the first Assembly, the Christian Union and its sister congregations had been wracked by fanaticism, falling prey to the excesses of itinerant preachers with more zeal than wisdom, and had had to regroup in May 1902. At that time, they changed their name to The Holiness Church. In 1907, at the second General Assembly, they adopted the name Church of God by which the denomination has subsequently been known.

From the time he joined in 1903, Tomlinson led the church in significant development. He moved to Cleveland, Tennessee, and became pastor of the church there. New congregations continued to spring up in surrounding towns and states. With a strong holiness emphasis and a powerful evangelistic impetus, men and women met responsive hearts everywhere they preached. Tomlinson himself seemed not to emphasize the baptism of the

Holy Spirit to any great extent until he received his personal Pentecost in 1907. This occurred during meetings conducted at his church by G. B. Cashwell, a North Carolina preacher who had received the Holy Spirit baptism at Azusa Street. During the intervening years Spurling, Bryant and others had continued to espouse the holiness and Pentecostal message. These men were respected spokesmen in the annual business meetings.

With rapid growth came the necessity of travel, oversight of new churches and organization. A church magazine, the *Church of God Evangel,* was initiated in 1910 and a Bible school, later known as Lee College, was established in Cleveland in 1918. Tomlinson was editor of the publication and president of the school. Each new step of development was authorized by the annual General Assembly and carried out by Tomlinson and a group of fellow ministers elected to lead the young denomination.

The aggressive church leader spearheaded the organization of a financial system that eventually caused his downfall in the church. Members of the church had practiced tithing from the earliest days of the church, with monies used to meet local church needs. The General Overseer (this was the title that identified the leader of the church) knew that some churches enjoyed substantially better income than others, so a system was devised and approved by the General Assembly for all tithes to be sent to Cleveland and disbursed from a central treasury. Tomlinson's management of the money and his strong personal leadership character caused difficulties that resulted in action by the General Assembly calling for him to step down from the top church post. Unwilling to vacate the office, the Overseer influenced about a third of the ministers to follow him, and he set up another church organization in Cleveland, which he continued to call the Church of God. The ensuing confusion in mail delivery and legal problems made a court case necessary, and the final decision required the Tomlinson group to choose another name for their church. It came to be called the Church of God of Prophecy.

When Tomlinson left, he was followed in the office of General Overseer by F. J. Lee, a popular and godly minister from Cleveland.

DISCOVERING THE GREAT COMMISSION

The first congregation of the Church of God gathered in 1886, but it was 1910, nearly 25 years later, before the first foreign missionary landed in another country. The church evidently understood and accepted its missions and church planting mandate from the beginning. However, it may correctly be observed that every step away from the mountains, through the southeastern states and eventually throughout the nation, was a missionary venture.

The saga of R. M. Evans, a retired Methodist preacher in Durant, Florida, who first carried the message of the church to the Bahama Islands in the West Indies, is chronicled by Charles W. Conn in *Where the Saints Have Trod.* This volume, a companion to the earlier denominational history, traces the beginning and growth of the foreign missions enterprise of the church.

Evans received the baptism of the Holy Spirit in a Florida camp meeting and shortly afterwards surrendered his Methodist ministerial credentials and his pension. Selling his house, he and his wife Ida traveled to Miami, booked passage to the Bahamas, and landed in Nassau during the first week of 1910. Joining fellowship with Edmund S. Barr, a Bahamian who had lived for awhile in Florida and had returned home, Evans began meetings which eventuated in the establishment of the Church of God. The new message was eagerly received and quickly spread from island to island. The earliest Nassau church began in 1910, but the oldest continuing congregation outside the United States is on a tiny island called Green Turtle Cay, off Abaco, in the northern sweep of the island chain.

The tentative beginning in the West Indies was the prelude to more ambitious undertakings in subsequent years. A number of eager preachers launched out in obedience to Christ's commission to take the gospel to all nations, but the church had not yet developed a sustaining financial plan that would insure them a base of support in the homeland. Several abortive church starts resulted. Later, in 1926, a Missions Board was established which, after passing through the throes of the Great Depression, placed a firm foundation under the missions vision of the fledgling denomination. Today missionaries and nearly 10,000 national pastors and church leaders work with Church of God congregations in 110 countries and territories.

The Church of God has been established in other countries basically in one of two ways: missionaries have initiated new works, in the manner of Evans in the Bahama Islands, and existing churches have elected to join or amalgamate with our church. A tireless traveler with dauntless zeal and international vision, Church of God minister J. H. Ingram was the principal representative of the denomination who established communication with independent missions and indigenous congregations, which resulted in their joining the church. For many years, especially during the 1930s and '40s, he journeyed to distant lands, orienting budding Pentecostal groups—results of the worldwide revival during the beginning years of the century—to Church of God doctrine and polity. His ambassadorial contacts resulted in church connections throughout Mexico, Central and South America, the West Indies, China, India and other lands.

In a few cases, large denominations have joined forces with the Church of God to become one in gospel witness. This has been true in South Africa, Indonesia and Rumania.

The church has wisely followed a course for many years that emphasizes the development of national leadership and ministry in each of its missions areas. Rather than building the church solely on North American missionaries, we have stressed the establishment of Bible schools and other training programs to prepare ministers indigenous to the area. This has the double benefit of ensuring a more likely hearing of the gospel and being somewhat less costly. Further, mature ministers from missions churches have themselves been sent as missionaries to yet other countries. God has blessed this approach to ministry by giving incredible growth.

DELEGATING THE WORK

The Church of God in its government has attempted to combine the best features of episcopal and congregational systems. In an episcopal structure, the church officials rule; in a congregational structure, the people make all the decisions in a democratic manner. Taking the Scriptures as a guide, but not finding a finely-detailed organizational procedure spelled out, the church combines both forms. As examples, the General Executive Committee (the General Overseer and his assistants) appoints members of all boards and committees, but they are themselves elected by the broad membership of the church. State overseers appoint local church pastors, but they are guided by a pastoral preference vote by members of the church.

About the same time that the *Evangel* was begun and mission work initiated, the church answered the need for state-level church administration. State overseers were appointed over seven southeastern states in 1911.

Supervision of the progress and expansion of the church at the state level included the programming of camp meetings, which to this day remain a backbone of the denominational activities. Although sophisticated auditoriums have largely taken the place of open-air tabernacles, the annual week-long summer gathering of ministers and lay people continues as a highlight of the church year. Bible teachers instruct in morning services and evangelists preach in the evening. General church officials and department leaders share fellowship, reports and promotional information. The bonds of friendship and fellowship are reinforced, and the experiences of worship impart new strength and inspiration.

To make its ministries more effective from the national headquarters, the church has developed specialized ministries in the form of departments and agencies, adding new ones periodically to meet fresh opportunities and challenges. Foreign missions was institutionalized with the appointment of a board of directors in 1926. At the same time, the publications and education ministries began to be guided by appointed boards. Youth and Christian education work had been managed for years by state-level leaders, but in 1946 a national board was formed and a director selected. Since the 1950s, boards and directors have been named for media ministries, evangelism, education (apart from the resident institutions), women's ministries, chaplains, lay affairs, public relations and stewardship.

To single out leaders and outstanding individuals who made significant contributions to this continuing developmental process would be difficult, if not impossible, and is certainly beyond the scope of this brief chapter. A representative person, however, whose record of ministry illustrates the levels at which contributions can be made in the church, is W. E. Johnson.

Johnson, a native Tennessean, began his ministry as a pastor in his home state, then served a total of 19 years as overseer of five states: Virginia, Florida, Alabama, Tennessee and Georgia. In two of the states he developed camp grounds, sprawling expanses where hugh open-air meeting places accommodated the crowds of thousands who flocked to the summer camp meeting in the heyday of their popularity. He was later pastor of the Tremont Avenue Church, in Greenville, South Carolina, one of the largest local congregations in the movement, and the Sulphur Springs, Florida, church.

He also served 12 years on the Executive Council, the highest decision-making body in the church besides the Assembly, composed for most of the years of our history of a Council of Twelve sitting with the Executive Committee. Additionally, he was a member of the World Missions Board from 1950 until 1968, holding the chairmanship for 12 of the 18 years, an office he was occupying in

1966 when the foreign membership total exceeded the United States membership total for the first time. Johnson's last appointment before his retirement was General Director of World Missions.

Any one of dozens of his colleagues might have been named here as a representative of the many distinguished leaders who made contributions in elective and appointive offices. One unusual characteristic marks his years in the church, however. He is probably one of the few ministers who has heard sermons from every General Overseer who has served the church, with the single exception of F. J. Lee (whose funeral he attended), from the beginning until the centennial celebration of the denomination.

The following men have been General Overseer in the years indicated:

1909-23	A. J. Tomlinson
1923-28	F. J. Lee
1928-35	S. W. Latimer
1935-44	J. H. Walker Sr.
1944-48	John C. Jernigan
1948-52	H. L. Chesser
1952-56	Zeno C. Tharp
1956-58	Houston R. Morehead
1958-62	James A. Cross
1962-66	Wade H. Horton
1966-70	Charles W. Conn
1970-72	R. Leonard Carroll
1972-74	Ray H. Hughes
1974-76	Wade H. Horton
1976-78	Cecil B. Knight

1978-82	Ray H. Hughes
1982-86	E. C. Thomas
1986-	Raymond E. Crowley

Men were elected to the top leadership post without limitation of service until the 1940s, when a tenure policy was placed into effect. A man may now serve a total of four years in any one position on the Executive Committee, and he may serve a total of eight years on the Committee.

J. H. Walker Sr. was the youngest man to hold the office, elected at age 35. Horton and Hughes are the only two to have been returned to the office again after their first tenure expired.

DECLARING OUR FAITH

A visit to a pastor's personal library today might reveal shelves heavy with materials written by Church of God leaders, teachers alnd scholars. We have produced books on doctrine and history, commentaries, sermon series, devotional collections, minister's manuals and study volumes, all based on Pentecostal theology. Further, the denominational publishing house prints thousands of commentaries and quarterly journals for Bible study use in Sunday schools.

It was not always so. Little writing for publication was done by the early generations of church leaders. A number of reasons explain this: The men of God communicated more by preaching than by writing. Many of the first preachers, although they were astute students of the Bible, were not trained in any formal way. The Bible school movement, which later dotted the land with teaching institutions, was itself in its infancy at the turn of the century. The Church of God started Lee College (first known as Bible Training School) in 1918, Northwest Bible College in 1938, International Bible College in 1939, West Coast Christian College in 1949, and East Coast Bible College in 1974. In the beginning years, most of the constituency was rural and poor. For the most part, they did not read much and did not attend college.

Spurling's first call for membership in the new organization had been for people who would accept the New Testament as their only rule of faith and practice. The guiding principle of belief would be individual study and interpretation of the Bible. Part of the blame for the cold ineffectiveness of many contemporary churches, they believed, was that these churches were bound by man-made creeds and traditions. A Spirit-enlivened body must avoid making the mistake of setting forth written creeds, they thought.

It was not long, however, until questions arose concerning beliefs and practices that needed to be addressed by the members together so they could speak with one voice about their convictions as a church. These matters have been the preoccupation of the General Assemblies. Two documents have resulted. One was a listing of teachings first set forth at the 1911 Assembly. This list addresses both theological and practical commitments of the church, and it has been added to and altered periodically through the years. While we have made no essential changes in matters of biblical doctrine in the one hundred years of the church's existence, we have found it necessary from time to time to restudy how these beliefs affect us in our interaction with the culture in which we live.

The other document is the Declaration of Faith, a profession of beliefs written in the form of theological statements, which was adopted at the 1948 Assembly. It is discussed in more detail in another chapter of this book.

Leaders of the Church of God have actively participated in the establishment of significant inter-church cooperative agencies, including the National Association of Evangelicals (1942), the World Pentecostal Fellowship (1947) and the Pentecostal Fellowship of North America (1948).

SUMMARY

The history of the Church of God is written in the biographies of men and women who have furnished general-level leadership and in the stories of thousands of grassroots pastors, evangelists and lay people who have preached the gospel, sacrificed and extended the church to its present boundaries.

Its best days are yet ahead, if Jesus tarries. Resources far beyond the dreams of the pioneers are now available. What is still needed is the vision and sense of God's guidance in our expansion to the ends of the earth.

CHAPTER REVIEW

1. What source can be identified as the definitive history of the Church of God?

2. Who is one of the most significant individuals to incorporate biblical precepts into personal and church life?

3. What is significant about the Azusa Street Mission?

4. From where did the name "General Assembly" originate?

5. By what other names has the Church of God been known?

6. How has the Church of God been established in other countries?

All That Believed Were Together

*E*ven a cursory glance at the Church of God reveals a complex structure.

More than a million members attend local churches outside the United States scattered throughout 110 countries and territories, worshiping in nearly 60 languages. More than half again that membership total gathers in North American churches in some 5,600 local congregations. If the growth rates that we have sustained in the past twenty years continue, we will exceed three million members by the year 2000. Thousands of pastors, evangelists and missionaries minister in the churches.

In the United States 52 state level administrators direct the affairs of the church, and in other countries eight superintendents coordinate the efforts of scores of national supervisors. From the headquarters offices in Cleveland, eight major departments plan, develop strategies and prepare programs and materials to facilitate the work of the church on the local level.

More than 60 schools, some of them with sprawling campuses and impressive faculties offering wide-ranging programs of study, operate to train ministers and lay people. Publishing enterprises generate millions of pieces of literature. Homes care for children who are orphans or come from broken homes. Rehabilitation centers work with troubled men and women.

It is extremely complex. How is it all organized?

A member of the church should be familiar with how the church is governed on three levels: the international, or general, organization; the state organization; and the local organization. The policies and procedures that guide our church on each level are contained in the *Book of Minutes* of the General Assembly. Measures and polity that have been adopted by our membership and ministers through the years are recorded in the *Minutes,* which is published in a new edition reflecting current changes each two years. Most of the material in the rest of this chapter comes from the *Minutes.* Members interested in further information may consult the *Minutes,* which includes a wealth of detail about matters of church discipline and practice.

Before surveying the organizational structure of the church, it is appropriate to discuss the scriptural and practical rationale for having church government.

WHY CHURCH ORGANIZATION?

The early church grew rapidly. Three thousand converts (Acts 2:41) were shortly followed by 5,000 men (Acts 4:4); then multitudes were added (Acts 5:14), and churches were multiplied (Acts 9:31). The movement quickly spread to other countries. Within a few years the church had moved to the boundaries of the Empire and beyond.

We look in vain to the Bible for any precise blueprint for church order. While we find the terms "bishop" and "elder" (the former borrowed from the Roman governmental system and denoting a regional civil overseer or a supervisor of a detachment of slaves; the latter taken from the Jewish setting, identifying senior members of the community who attended to civil and religious matters), there is no precision of usage of the titles in the church. "Overseer" (as it is translated in some English versions, e.g., Acts 20:28) is the same Greek word as "bishop," *episkopos.*

What apparently happened is that when the earliest New Testament churches began with predominantly Jewish constituency, the leaders were called elders. When the setting was primarily Gentile, the name "bishop" or "overseer" was employed. Paul and Luke seemed to use the titles interchangeably (compare Acts 20:17 with Acts 20:28). Besides these particular titles for officers in the church, the epistles also identify individuals called "deacons" and "helpers."

If exact details about local structures is lacking, it is quite clear that an associational cooperative arrangement existed—what we in the Church of God call central government.

The Jerusalem Christians gathered in homes for fellowship and instruction (Acts 2:46; 5:42). Several thousand believers made up the church membership, so it is evident that many churches existed. Yet the church is always identified in the singular, not in the plural, as in Acts 8:1-3; 11:22; 12:5; and other verses. The same observation may be made about the church in other places besides Jerusalem (Acts 11:26; 13:1; 14:27).

All of the churches together seem to have been united under the oversight and leadership of the apostolic band (Acts 11:1; 15:2; 21:18). The churches everywhere accepted the judgment of the Jerusalem Council (Acts 15) with regard to a vexing problem they were confronting. Even in benevolent matters, the first-century church practiced a mutual relationship.

As the years passed and the Roman Empire's civil government began to interfere with the governing of the church, a rigid and powerful hierarchy developed that ultimately influenced the complete secularization of what was intended to be a spiritual organization.

A pendulum swing away from the excesses of the Roman Catholic Church system at the time of the Reformation conditioned many Protestant churches to look for justification for completely autonomous local congregations, but the New Testament knows nothing of independent churches unrelated to the others.

Central government allows great progress for the church. Large achievements requiring substantial investments of money and personnel are possible, which would be beyond the scope of a lone congregation. Missionaries can be sent and homeless children attended. Spiritual safeguards are in place. False teachers and unfaithful ministers may be identified and disciplined. Accountability and submission, scriptural requirements for men of God, are provided. Cooperative decision-making—the wisdom of a multitude of counselors—is possible. Although dangers sometimes accrue to centrally-governed denominations—stagnation, perpetuation of inept leadership, unwieldy bureaucracy, reluctance to change—these can be overcome with spiritual participation by rank and file ministers and members. The benefits of the system far outweigh the alternatives.

ORGANIZATION AT THE INTERNATIONAL LEVEL

The Church of God conducts a biennial General Assembly that meets to consider matters relating to the teachings and government of the church. These large conventions, attended by thousands, meet in different cities; recent assemblies have been held in Dallas, Kansas City, Atlanta and Fort Worth. The General Assembly is the highest body of the church. Any member who wishes—layperson or minister—may attend. The Assembly elects general church officials according to procedures defined in the bylaws that are written in the *Book of Minutes.* Principal officials are the members of the General Executive Committee and directors of key departments of the denomination. Another group, called the Council of Eighteen, is elected by the ordained ministers present at the General Assembly. The Council of Eighteen, sitting in joint session with the Executive Committee, comprises the Executive Council.

Five men constitute the Executive Committee. These men reside in Cleveland, Tennessee, where the church's international offices are located, during their terms of office. They are nominated by vote of the ordained ministers of the church and elected by the delegates to the General Assembly. The five officers are the General Overseer, three Assistant General Overseers and the General Secretary-Treasurer. They are limited as to how long they may remain in office. Their duties are spelled out in the *Minutes*. Generally speaking, these five men furnish leadership and supervise the day-to-day work of the denomination.

The Council of Eighteen is comprised of ordained ministers who meet periodically with the Executive Committee to conduct the business of the denomination that must be attended to between the biennial assemblies. A set number of them must be pastors and at least two must be from outside the United States.

Work at the Cleveland headquarters is performed by various departments. Eight principal departments are headed by directors and guided by boards. Numerous service auxiliaries and agencies support the functioning of the denomination. The directors—some elected by the General Assembly and some appointed by the Executive Committee—and their staffs are full-time employees of the church. The boards that guide their work are constituted of men and women who have other jobs or ministries and meet periodically in relationship to the work of the department.

The main departments are World Missions, Evangelism and Home Missions, Youth and Christian Education, Editorial and Publications, General Education, Radio and Television, Ladies Ministries and Benevolence. Other agencies and offices include Public Relations, Business and Records, Pensions, Insurance, Lay Affairs, Chaplains Commission and Cross-Cultural Ministries.

The directors of departments meet together regularly with the Executive Committee, sitting together as the Board of Church Ministries, to plan the work of the denomination. Additionally, one of the men on the Executive Committee is assigned to meet as a liaison member with each board to further ensure interdepartmental communication and cooperation.

One of the chief responsibilities of the Executive Committee is appointing members of the departmental boards. Another key task is appointing state overseers.

Funding for international ministries operated from the general executive offices is provided by local churches. Each month the local churches send a report of their activities to the church headquarters in Cleveland, including an amount of money equal to six percent of their tithe income. (After 1990 the amount is five percent.) The Executive Council apportions the income to the various departments in the form of annual budgets. Careful safeguards and audits by agencies outside the departments ensure that monies are properly administered. With this system the Church of God is able to start new churches, operate benevolent agencies, assist retired and disabled ministers, underwrite evangelists, sponsor colleges and Bible schools, broadcast and telecast the gospel via media, and promote scores of programs through its various departments which help the local churches become more effective in evangelism and nurture.

Most of the ministry offices are located in Cleveland, Tennessee. This county-seat town about one hundred miles north of Atlanta and 30 miles east of Chattanooga became the early center of church operations because of its proximity to the rural mountain area where the movement began. It is a pleasant but fast-paced community of some 35,000 residents and diverse business, educational and industrial interests.

A handsome four-story executive office building on beautifully landscaped grounds on Cleveland's principal thoroughfare houses most of the church's administrative functions. A large complex in another part of town contains the church's publishing house. Still another structure accommodates the recording studios and offices of the media ministries. Lee College, the principal educational institution of the church, occupies about 35 acres near the downtown area in a residential section of some of Cleveland's oldest and finest homes. The School of Theology and North Cleveland Church (the denomination's oldest continually existing church) adjoin the Lee campus.

ORGANIZATION AT THE STATE LEVEL

The chief executive officer of the Church of God in each state is the State Overseer. State overseers are appointed by the General Executive Committee of the denomination at the time of the biennial General Assembly. Overseers may serve two consecutive two-year terms in one state. The Executive Committee takes into consideration a vote from the ministers in the state when they name the overseer.

The term "state" is used by the church, although specifically speaking it may not be a precise designation. Some states with large numbers of churches are divided into two jurisdictions, each with its own "state" overseer (e.g., North Georgia and South Georgia, Eastern North Carolina and Western North Carolina). In states where the membership is small, adjoining states are sometimes grouped together under one "state" overseer (e.g., Southern New England).

Duties of a state overseer are broad-ranging. He directs the growth of the churches in his state, planning and implementing evangelistic programs and spearheading the establishment of new congregations. He appoints district overseers and local church pastors. He approves local church building programs. He conducts statewide conventions; these usually include a camp meeting or convention in the summer months and a prayer and evangelism conference in the winter months. The overseer also moderates meetings of the state council. His other duties are detailed in the *Minutes* of the General Assembly.

Most states have a full-time minister who is Director of Youth and Christian Education. It is his job to promote and implement programs of Christian education in the local churches. He usually plans summer camps for children and young people, promotes the establishment and effective operation of Sunday school and Family Training Hour in each local church, directs youth missions fundraising programs and otherwise ministers in the areas of youth and education. He works with a board elected by the state ministers and he is supervised by the state overseer.

Some states have a State Evangelism Director who works with the state overseer in programs of church growth and new church planting.

Each state also has a State Education Board, a group of men who coordinate programs of ministerial and lay training and enrichment.

The State Overseer moderates meetings of the State Council, a board of ministers elected by their colleagues, who labor with him in planning and evaluating the work of the church in the state. They meet, usually monthly or quarterly, to deal with budgetary matters and other concerns of the overseer. Each state is divided geographically into districts, which may contain from two to 25 churches. The overseer appoints a minister in the area, normally pastor of one of the churches, as district overseer. The district overseer serves as an assistant and coworker with the overseer in dealing with the concerns of the local churches.

ORGANIZATION AT THE LOCAL LEVEL

The heart of the Church of God beats in its local congregations. Structures at the state and general levels exist to coordinate and maximize ministries and give overall leadership, but the local church is the focal point of the denomination.

The pastor is the leader of the local church. He is the man who must give accountability to God for his members. He is held responsible by the church leadership for the well-being of his congregation. He is chosen and affirmed by the membership of the church to be their pastor, and he assumes the pastoral office upon appointment by the State Overseer.

Pastoral appointments were once made on an annual basis, then changed to biennial. In 1966 they were extended to four years. Recently the church voted to name pastors for indefinite appointments. The church has noted that churches which frequently change pastors usually do not experience growth, while the ones which have long-term pastors grow at a better rate.

The governmental structure encourages a state overseer to monitor periodically the growth and decline of the churches under his supervision. He has the prerogative of contacting pastors and churches about change when he judges it in the best interest of either. Local churches may request the overseer to give them opportunity to vote for change.

Local churches conduct the business of the church in meetings called conferences. They are of two types— regular and called. Regular conferences consist of the total membership, men and women; called conferences, which may be convened by district or state overseers to attend to specific items of business, consist of male members. If a church wishes to have a Church and Pastor's Council, the regular conference may elect a group of men, the size of the council determined by a membership formula set forth in the *Minutes*. The council works with the pastor in the institution and direction of local church programs. Generally, they furnish spiritual leadership to the congregation, approve the disbursement of funds and oversee the provision and maintenance of physical properties. The pastor sets the meetings of the Council and serves as its chairman.

Each local church has a church clerk, elected biennially by the membership. A man or woman may hold the office. He or she keeps records of the membership and finances and makes monthly reports to state and general offices. Duties of the church clerk are defined in the *Minutes.*

A local church's financial system is based on the tithe. All members of the Church of God should pay tithes, ten percent of their income, to the church where they are members. This is an ancient, God-inspired program of ensuring the ongoing of the worship and service of God. It was practiced by men of God in the Old Testament prior to institution of the law of Moses; it was demanded of the people of God by the Mosaic standard; and it was observed in the time of Christ. Jesus himself blessed the practice of tithing, almost incidentally, when He commended those who did it. The New Testament teaches proportionate contributions; ten percent is the biblical portion. Local Churches of God, in the tradition of the New Testament church, afford their members opportunity for giving, above and beyond the tithe, for worthwhile purposes such as the relief of the poor and hungry, sending missionaries and caring for widows and orphans.

The ministries of the local church are actuated through agencies and individuals in place for specific service. Perhaps the most familiar and most visible of these is the Sunday school.

First organized in England more than two hundred years ago and quickly spreading to America, the Sunday school has traditionally been the seat of Bible training in the local church. In a typical school, the classes are organized on the basis of grade and age, with teachers assigned for one-year periods. The Church of God uses a curriculum that takes students through the whole Bible in a seven-year cycle. When the cycle is repeated, the literature is changed to reflect a varied approach to the lessons. Increased Bible knowledge is the goal of the Sunday school.

Family Training Hour, held on Wednesday nights in most churches, is a program providing training in Christian living and serving. Its classes emphasize "how-to" aspects of discipleship, such as Bible study, prayer, witnessing and related subjects. Youth groups may meet in connection with Family Training Hour or may schedule other meeting times.

Many churches have choirs that practice on nonservice nights to prepare music for the Sunday services, although smaller churches prefer choirs that sing spontaneously.

Churches that are able to pay the salaries of other staff members will employ assistants to the pastor, often specialists in Christian education, evangelism, music or youth work. About 20 percent of the churches in the denomination have individuals besides the pastor on the church payroll.

A relatively new ministry in the Church of God is Christian day schools, in which the church offers a substitute for public education. Nearly three hundred local churches sponsor such schools, ranging in size from a handful of students to more than five hundred. They emphasize traditional educational goals with the extra dimension of a spiritual perspective.

THE MINISTRY OF THE LOCAL CHURCH

The denomination has not developed a job description for pastors or a checklist of ministry involvement for local churches, probably because of our conviction that the New Testament is our rule of faith and practice. A study of the Scriptures furnishes guidelines to let us know our reponsibilities and opportunities.

The church is charged with three basic categories of ministries: worship, which is God-directed; edification and education, which is us-oriented; and evangelism and service, which is other-centered. Here is how these ministries may be carried out from the local church.

Ministries to God

There is a sense in which the church may be appropriately called the Temple of God because we are charged to cultivate in our members true worship and spiritual service (John 4:23, 24, 1 Corinthians 3:16, 17, Ephesians 2:19-22). No certain format governs the shape of a service of worship. Our culture, background and traditions influence the way we interpret scriptural injunctions to worship. Some, for example, will be comfortable in quietness while others will feel it appropriate to clap their hands. The primary test of a worship experience is simply, "Did we enter the presence of God and sense His awe and greatness?" This may be done in a cathedral or a grass hut or outdoors; it may be accompanied by a pipe organ or guitar or no accompaniment at all.

Ministries to the Church

As we meet together for worship and service, part of what should happen is the cultivation of true fellowship and mutual care among the people of God (Acts 2:42, 47; 4:32, 33, Ephesians 2:20-22, 1 John). This is evidenced when there is a general sense of fraternity within the church, when people call each other "Brother" and "Sister" not out of convention but out of caring; when there are tangible demonstrations such as a desire to spend time with other church families or to reach out to those who are suffering.

Edifying and perfecting the children of God form part of our ministry. These words imply a kind of "building up" of people, by training and equipping them for meaningful service. This can be measured when there are evidences of fruitful ministry being practiced by members (Acts 20:27, 28, Ephesians 4:11-16, 1 Peter 5:1-3).

Part of our service to fellow Church of God members is to bear the weak in faith, care for the fallen and help to restore them to Christian victory (John 15:1-7, Romans 15:1-15, Galatians 6:1, Colossians 2:16-23, 1 Thessalonians 2:7-16). This is nowhere more apparent than when we see lapsed or nonattending members come back to church after having left it. The human, worldly tendency is to leave them to themselves; the

Christian response is to seek them out and express loving concern.

Ministries to the World

Sharing the good news of Christ with men and women who do not know Him and bringing them into fellowship with Him and into responsible church membership is a priority goal for the Church of God (Matthew 5:13-14; 28:18-20, Luke 24:45-49, Acts 1:8). We can know for certain if we are faithful to this purpose of the church if new converts are being added to the church.

The people of the Church of God have a "salt" and "light' function in the world. We are called upon to be a judge and conscience of culture and movements (Matthew 5:13-15, Philippians 2:14-16, 1 John 4:1). While we may not feel capable of taking on the power structures of evil in this world, we can voice our opinions and concerns to the circle of opeople whom we might influence and not be quiet when we should speak. Evil flourishes when good men and women do nothing.

Pastors and scholars may add to this list, but these are some of the basic values and emphases of the Church of God. We are organized on general, state and local levels in such a way as to be able to carry out these ministries.

A church that ministers to God, to the saints and to the world is a church that pleases the Lord of the Church.

CHAPTER REVIEW ⸻

1. On what three levels is the church governed; what source of policies and procedures is used to guide each level?
2. Identify the following terms:
   General Assembly
   Executive Committee
   Council of Eighteen
3. Identify the eight primary departments of the church.

4. How is an overseer assigned to a state? What are his responsibilities?

5. Differentiate between regular and called conferences.

CHAPTER 4

The Apostles' Doctrine

"*W*hat does your church believe?" is one of the first questions to be expected of the curious who visit a local congregation of the Church of God. "Be ready always to give an answer to every man that asketh you a reason of the hope that is in you" (1 Peter 3:15) is the biblical guideline for replying to questions about belief.

THE BASIS OF FAITH

The Holy Bible constitutes the basis of Church of God faith. The Old Testament is the record of God's revelation of Himself and His dealings particularly with the Jews, whom He chose to live in a special relationship with Him and to carry out the mission of revealing Him to the world. The New Testament tells about the life and ministry of Christ and the establishment and development of the Christian church; in it the focus moves away from Israel to all men who accept the message of Christ and become His followers. The New Testament, then, is the primary source of what we believe.

Throughout the history of the Christian church, attempts have been made to extract from Scripture the essentials of faith and reduce them to simple statements

67

of belief. This is salutary and beneficial, for the Bible itself counsels us that we should all speak the same things and not have divisions among us. The Apostles' Creed and the numerous credenda that have followed it are evidences of the value of compacting complex and voluminous truth into manageable, memorizable format. The danger related to creeds is apparent: it is possible to allow them to degenerate into words, familiar and repeated, but meaningless when related to real life. Most of us have had the sad experience of hearing crowds mumble in unison eloquent affirmations of faith, only to observe subsequent lifestyles that give lie to what they have recited. For this reason many pastors and church leaders in the early years of our denomination resisted, even were antagonistic to, the idea of formulating the basic theological thought of the church into a statement of faith. This was finally accomplished more than a half-century after the church's initiation. The denomination's 1948 Assembly approved the Declaration of Faith.

The following pages will introduce the Declaration of Faith, item by item, and state essentially what is meant by each affirmation. It is exceedingly difficult to attempt a brief exposition for two reasons. Each item, on its own, has been the subject of many books; therefore, to try to capsulize them in a few paragraphs is presumptuous in the first place. Second, any incursion into doctrinal matters, by nature of the effort, requires introduction of theological terminology. Religious vocabulary sometimes means one thing to one person and something different to another. The following statements are necessarily brief and do not pretend to examine all aspects of the issues. No divine inspiration is claimed for these pages! A good case can be made, however, for the use of these explanations as a beginning point for answering the question, "What does your church believe?" Local Church of God pastors can supplement this section, upon request, for readers who wish to explore particular subjects in greater detail. Further, scriptures pertinent to each item are listed following each discussion for those who wish to pursue Bible studies on specific items.

[NOTE: *In this chapter the designation "man" is used in a number of instances to refer to humankind in general, male and female. Inclusive language, the repeated use of "he and she" or "him and her" might have been better, but at times it seems cumbersome or awkward. Readers should understand that both men and women are included in the references.*]

THE DECLARATION OF FAITH

We believe:

1. In the verbal inspiration of the Bible.

Christendom has taken several positions regarding the Bible. Some men maintain that it is an inspired book in the same way that Shakespeare or Milton was inspired. Others claim a higher merit for it but hesitate short of declaring its full inspiration and authority. We believe that God himself inspired its writing by revealing truth to men and guiding them to faithfully record what He revealed.

Natural truth may be intrinsically discovered by scientific investigation, but supernatural truth may be known only if it is revealed by God. We accept the Bible as the record of that revelation. It does not contradict truth in the natural realm.

God's revelation is trustworthy and dependable and should be used as the foundation for all that we believe. The 66 books that make up our Bible were penned by some 40 different writers over a period of about 1500 years, yet taken together they comprise a remarkable unity that is difficult of explanation apart from divine inspiration. The personalities of the writers were not submerged, for the various books bear the distinctive stamp of their human authors (Paul's epistles are typically complex and involved, for example, while Peter's are generally more simple in syntactical structure); but the affirmation of the Book about itself, confirmed by the witness of fulfilled prophecy and centuries of personal application, is that "All scripture is given by inspiration of God" (2 Timothy 3:16).

Scriptures for further study: 2 Peter 1:20, 21. Matthew 5:18. 1 Peter 1:10, 11. John 5:39, 46. Luke 24:27. Psalm 118:89. Deuteronomy 31:24. Deuteronomy 6:7, 8. Acts 28:23. Psalm 119:105. Psalm 19:7. 2 Timothy 3:16. Isaiah 55:10, 11.

2. In one God, eternally existing in three persons; namely, the Father, Son, and Holy Ghost.

Another way of making this claim is to call ourselves trinitarian, or say we believe in the Trinity. Neither the word *trinity* nor the word *persons,* in the sense it is used here, appears in Scripture, but we employ it to convey what the Bible teaches.

God, the Father and Creator, is God; Jesus Christ, the Son, is God; and the Holy Spirit is God. Having confessed that truth, however, we have not said that three gods exist. God is one and yet is three persons, all equally divine, eternal and unchangeable. An element of mystery remains that God is one existing in three perons. Scripture affirms that God has manifested himself as Father, Son and Holy Spirit as He has eternally existed and clearly teaches that the Father begets, the Son is begotten and the Holy Spirit proceeds from the Father to the Son. The Father, Son and Holy Spirit are distinct in person and office, but they are so uniquely and perfectly one in character and unity that they constitute the one God. Only by the help of the Holy Spirit can we understand that God is one being existing in three persons from all eternity. Even then the doctrine of trinity defies ordinary logic and human understanding. At this point we do not say, as some have declared, "Well, since we cannot understand it, we reject it." Instead, we accept the testimony of the Bible claiming unequivocally that the Father is God, the Son is God, and the Holy Spirit is God; and, there is one God.

Scriptures for further study: 2 Corinthians 13:14. 1 Peter 1:2. 1 John 5:7, 8. Genesis 1:26. Ephesians 2:18, 22. Ephesians 4:4, 5. Matthew 1:22, 23. John 1:1. John 20:28. Acts 20:28. 1 Timothy 3:16. 1 John 1:1, 2. John 14:7-11. Acts 5:3, 4. 1 Corinthians 3:16, 17. 1 Corinthians 6:19, 20.

3. **That Jesus Christ is the only begotten Son of the Father, conceived of the Holy Ghost and born of the Virgin Mary. That Jesus was crucified, buried and raised from the dead. That he ascended into heaven and is today at the right hand of the Father as the Intercessor.**

The New Testament affirms that Jesus is deity. He pre-existed in heaven, then was incarnated as a baby born of Mary, a young Jewish woman, while she was yet a virgin. His conception was the act of the Holy Spirit. He grew up in the home of Joseph and Mary. He began a public ministry of teaching and healing when He was 30 years old. About three years later He was executed on a cross by the Romans, based on charges made by the Jews. His dead body was placed in a tomb, but three days later He was raised to life. After a brief period of further ministry and teaching to His disciples, He ascended bodily into heaven where He remains today as the advocate and intercessor for His people.

Scriptures for further study: Matthew 1:18-25. Luke 1:26-42. Matthew 16:21-23. Mark 8:31-33. Luke 9:22. John 12:32-34. Matthew 12:39, 40. John 7:33, 34. Matthew 27:35, 36, 59, 60. Acts 7:55, 56. Colossians 3:1. Hebrews 4:14-16. Hebrews 7:19-25.

4. **That all have sinned and come short of the glory of God and that repentance is commanded of God for all and necessary for forgiveness of sins.**

As God created them, man and woman were in His image and likeness, possessing intelligence, conscience and will, capable of exercising dominion for God over the earth. Man's response to temptation, which came from the devil manifesting himself in the form of a serpent, was to doubt God's Word and disobey His commandment. The result was the entrance of sin into man's experience and into the world.

Sin separates man from God, mars the divine image and prevents man's entrance into heaven. God provides reconciliation through faith in Jesus Christ; but to benefit from God's provision, man must repent. Repentance is a change of mind and a change of direction. It is evidenced by confession, and it procures cleansing and forgiveness.

Scriptures for further study: Genesis 1:26, 31. Genesis 3:1-7. Psalm 8:4-8. Joshua 24:15. Luke 12:47, 48. Romans 1:21-31. Romans 3:9-18. Romans 5:12-19. Hebrews 4:15. Mark 1:15. Luke 13:3. Acts 3:19. Titus 2:11. Romans 10:13-15. Titus 3:5-7.

5. **That justification, regeneration, and the new birth are wrought by faith in the blood of Jesus Christ.**

Justification is a term taken from the legal setting. In a court of law, judgment is made and sentence is pronounced; however, an accused may be "justified," or declared righteous, if the charges against him are removed. Jesus Christ did exactly that for all men when He died a substitutionary death on the cross. The shedding of His blood paid the price necessary to satisfy the righteous Judge. His act declares the accused "not guilty," excludes all possibility of condemnation and restores all the privileges due to those who have kept the law. When we are justified, it is—in the eyes of God—"just-as-if-I'd" never sinned.

Regeneration, or being born again, is an act of the Holy Spirit whereby the fallen nature of man is morally and spiritually renewed and man is restored to a personal relationship with God. This occurs by the grace of God and happens when a sinner repents and trusts in Jesus Christ alone for his salvation.

Scriptures for further study: 1 John 1:9. Romans 5:1. Isaiah 55:6, 7. John 16:8. John 1:11-13. John 3:3-7. Ephesians 2:1. Colossians 2:13. Romans 8:33. 1 Corinthians 6:13. Romans 1:17. Hebrews 4:2.

6. In sanctification, subsequent to the new birth, through faith in the blood of Christ; through the Word, and by the Holy Ghost.

The Bible teaches that man should live a life of holiness, without which he cannot see God. This is what is meant by sanctification. It has a twofold aspect: it means, (1) to separate or set apart from ordinary to special usage, and (2) to cleanse or purify.

The sanctifying work is performed by the Holy Spirit as an act of separating and cleansing, and it continues with the cooperation of man as he fulfills his responsibility in the covenant of grace. Christ begins to cleanse in the process of salvation, and He continues to cleanse as man surrenders his heart and life to God. Justification may be thought of as what God does for us, while sanctification is what God does in us. We are first placed into a right relationship with God. Then the fruit of that relationship is exhibited in a sanctified life.

Scriptures for further study: Romans 6:1-13. Ephesians 4:20-25. Colossians 3:9-11. James 1:21. Romans 5:2. Hebrews 13:12. 1 Corinthians 1:30. 1 Thessalonians 4:3.

7. Holiness to be God's standard of living for His people.

Holiness is the result of the sanctifying experience. It reflects the idea of being set apart from what is common and unclean and being consecrated to what is pure. God is described as holy, certain objects and institutions are holy, and men are said to be holy. Holiness is regarded as separateness and ethical righteousness.

Holiness is the status of those who have been joined to Christ. The actions and moral quality of life of those who have been renewed by the indwelling Christ and consent to be ruled by Him are identified with the term *holiness.* Holiness implies the moral impossibility of continuing in sin while living for God.

Holiness came to identify a nineteeth-century movement within the Christian church that aimed to reclaim testimonies of victory over sin in the lives of Christians. Because of abuses of the doctrine, resistance by nominal Christians and a perceived legalism on the part of many who sought holiness of character, the word took on a pejorative note. Holiness, however, is a biblical concept, a beautiful idea and is the fundamental attribute of God. It is His desire for His people.

Scriptures for further study: Luke 1:75. 1 Thessalonians 4:7. Hebrews 12:14. John 15:16. John 17:6. Ephesians 1:4. Ephesians 2:10. 2 Thessalonians 2. 2:13. Hebrews 10:28, 29.

8. In the baptism of the Holy Ghost subsequent to a clean heart.

God wills for His people to be filled with the Holy Spirit. Jesus prophecied the initial filling on Pentecost using the phrase, "You shall be *baptized* with the Holy Spirit not long from now," so the Church of God uses the term "baptism of the Spirit" to identify the experience. Perhaps the best literal translation of the Greek is "baptism in the Spirit."

Holy Spirit baptism can happen only to saved individuals. The New Testament pattern reveals several incidences of this truth. The disciples were saved, then baptized in the Spirit on the Day of Pentecost. Philip preached in Samaria and his hearers were saved; later Peter and John visited the new converts and they received the Holy Spirit. The disciples of John interviewed by Paul at Ephesus had been baptized unto repentance, but when Paul prayed for them they received the Holy Spirit.

The purpose of the baptism in the Spirit is to endow believers with spiritual power to enable them to witness and to render spiritual service. Every believer is indwelled by the Spirit at the time of salvation (indeed, his conviction and new birth are works of the Spirit), but Spirit baptism is something more.

[NOTE: The King James Version of the Bible sometimes translates the Greek word *pneuma* as "ghost" and sometimes as "spirit." The newer translations consistently render it "spirit," which is the more exact meaning of the word. The Greek uses another word, *phantasma* (as in Mark 6:49), for "ghost."]

Scriptures for further study: Luke 24:49. Acts 1:4, 8. 1 Corinthians 12:1-31. Acts 10:44-46. Acts 11:14-16. John 7:37-39. John 14:16, 26. John 16:7. Romans 6:17. Ephesians 5:18. 1 Corinthians 2:14. John 20:22.

9. In speaking with other tongues as the Spirit gives utterance and it is the initial evidence of the baptism of the Holy Ghost.

When individuals receive the baptism in the Holy Spirit, witnesses note obvious signs of His entrance into their lives. Often exuberant joy and complete abandonment to God's will marks the moment. Other signs may be attendant, but only one evidence is universally present in the biblical instances of Spirit baptism, either overtly mentioned or indirectly adduced: speaking in tongues.

Speaking in tongues was first heard in the Upper Room, where all the people spoke the same language and did not need other languages to make themselves intelligible. It was the sign of the Baptism.

When Cornelius and his household received the Baptism, they spoke with tongues, according to Acts 10. The disciples of John, whose account of Spirit baptism is given in Acts 19, spoke in tongues. On at least two other occasions where people received the baptism in the Spirit (the Samaritans in Acts 8 and Paul in Acts 9), the strong implication is that they spoke in tongues.

Speaking in tongues as the initial evidence of the baptism in the Holy Spirit should not be confused with the gift of tongues, which is mentioned elsewhere in the New Testament.

Scriptures for further study: Mark 16:17. Acts 2:1-4. Acts 8:14-17. Acts 9:17. Acts 10:44-46. Acts 19:5-7. 1 Corinthians 14:18. 1 Corinthians 12-14. Acts 2:39. Hebrews 2:4.

10. In water baptism by immersion and all who repent should be baptized in the name of the Father, and of the Son, and of the Holy Ghost.

Water baptism was practiced in New Testament times as an outward, physical symbol of an inward, spiritual experience. Repentant sinners had bowed in the presence of God, were forgiven of their sins and were imparted a new nature. This was regeneration, or the new birth, as Jesus called it. As a testimony of their inner cleansing, they subjected themselves to a public immersion in water to represent what had happened in their lives.

Baptism in the first-century church was performed by the baptizer entering the water with the candidate, dipping him beneath the water and raising him up. In later centuries some churches altered the mode of baptism by pouring water over the candidate's head or by sprinkling water, but the Church of God continues to follow the New Testament pattern.

The formula spoken by the baptizing minister is the one instructed by Christ in His parting Great Commission— ". . . baptizing them in the name of the Father, and of the Son, and of the Holy Ghost" (Matthew 28:19).

Scriptures for further study: Matthew 28:19. Acts 10:47, 48. Romans 6:4. Acts 20:21. Hebrews 10:22. Acts 8:36. John 3:23. Colossians 2:12. Matthew 3:16. Acts 2:38, 41. Acts 16:14, 15, 32, 33.

11. Divine healing is provided for all in the atonement.

Sickness and suffering are part of the curse that is upon the world because of sin. They did not originate from God but from Satan. At times in our present experience, God uses the dark night of suffering to teach His children, but there is no scripture to indicate that

He ever places sickness upon anyone. Christ was made a curse for us, in the terminology of the Bible, that we might go free from the curse of sin.

During His earthly ministry, Jesus himself healed, and He committed the ministry of healing to His disciples and to the church. His final words included a commission to lay hands on the sick and a promise that they would recover.

Like salvation, which is also provided for us in His atoning work, healing is appropriated by faith.

Scriptures for further study: Acts 10:38. Luke 13:11-17. Hebrews 2:14, 15. 1 John 3:8. Galatians 3:10-14. Matthew 8:16, 17. 1 Peter 2:24. Matthew 10:7, 8. Luke 10:9. Acts 5:12, 15. Luke 7:21, 22. James 5:14-16.

12. In the Lord's Supper and washing of the saints' feet.

Besides water baptism, the Church of God observes two other ordinances, the Lord's Supper and Foot Washing.

The Lord's Supper, instituted by Christ himself, is symbolic of His broken body and shed blood. Each time we eat the bread and drink the fruit of the vine, we confess three great truths: We demonstrate in a tangible fashion that we share the divine nature of our Lord (this is a demonstration and does not suggest that the bread and cup are anything more than symbolic in their significance); we memorialize the suffering and death of the Lord; and we express our hope of His second coming.

Foot washing is practiced in obedience to the specific instructions of the Lord. It is an act that illustrates humility and a willingness to follow Christ's model of servanthood in our relationships with other people. But the primary signficance of it lies in the fact that just as baptism and the Lord's Supper are rooted in the atoning death of Christ, so also is this ordinance. Before His sacrificial death our Lord provided the disciples with a reminder of continuing forgiveness available to the believer. The washing of the saints' feet is a spiritually strengthening experience and should be observed in the worship of God, for it is a visual reminder that grace is available to believers.

Scriptures for further study: Luke 22:17-20. 1 Corinthians 11:22-29. Matthew 26:29. John 6:48-58. 1 Corinthians 10:16, 17. John 13:4-17. 1 Timothy 5:9, 10.

13. In the premillenial second coming of Jesus. First, to resurrect the righteous dead and to catch away the living saints to Him in the air. Second, to reign on the earth a thousand years.

The Church of God takes literally the prophecy of Revelation that a thousand years of peace will precede a great, final battle in which the powers of evil will be ultimately defeated. Prior to the Millennium (as the thousand-year period is called), Jesus will come to the earth.

He will come in the air. At that time, all Christians who have died will be returned to life. About the same moment, all living Christians will be received up from the earth into heaven with Him (an event the church calls the "Rapture," an interpretation of the biblical phrase "caught away").

Following the Rapture and a seven-year period, which will be marked by great joy in heaven but great trouble on earth, Christ will return to the earth and set up His kingdom. Under His rule, the world will enjoy a thousand years of holiness and peace.

Scriptures for further study: 1 Thessalonians 4:15-17. 2 Thessalonians 2:1. 1 Corinthians 15:52. Romans 8:23. Titus 2:13. 2 Thessalonians 1:7-10. Jude 14, 15. Revelation 5:10. Revelation 19:11-21. Acts 1:9-11.

14. In the bodily resurrection; eternal life for the righteous, and eternal punishment for the wicked.

Christians who have died will be resurrected at the time of Christ's returning. They will be judged according to the works they have done to determine the rewards they will receive in heaven. Sinners will remain in the grave until the final day of judgment when they will be brought to life to face their condemnation.

Human language falls short of being able to describe the post-resurrection state of the believer and the unbeliever. Heaven's grandeur is described in Revelation 21 and 22. Earlier in the same book the horrors of the lake of fire, the final home of sinners, are told. The two situations stand in stark contrast. The Bible teaches that the abode to which men are consigned at judgment will be their dwelling place throughout eternity.

Scriptures for further study: John 5:28, 29. Acts 24:15. Revelation 20:5, 6. Matthew 25:46. Luke 18:30. John 10:28. Romans 6:22, 23. 1 John 5:11-13. Mark 3:29. 2 Thessalonians 1:8, 9. Revelation 20:10-15. Revelation 21:8.

COMMITMENT TO PRACTICAL HOLINESS

Right belief issues forth in right living. The Church of God believes that the Christian's lifestyle is affected by his or her commitment to Christ. In an attempt to provide guidelines for how this life should be lived out in practical ways, the church has produced a listing of teachings that have been prominent since our early beginnings and have been modified at times over the years.

Arriving at a statement of practical commitments and reviewing them from time to time for change as needed has been difficult for the church and will probably continue to be difficult until Jesus comes. The church has earnestly attempted to steer a clear path between two opposite temptations.

On the one hand has been the opinion of some among us that the church should not, under any circumstances, set down rules and dictums. The Holy Spirit is the believer's indwelling guide, they maintain; therefore, man-made rules and lists apart from the Bible as it is written should be avoided at all costs. So strong was this fear in the earliest days that the record of the first deliberations of the church included a statement expressing hope that nothing that was written down would ever form the basis for a body of belief which would result in a new denomination!

At the opposite extreme has been the temptation to try to produce lists of rules that would cover every possible situation of life. Individuals with fervent zeal, sensing the dangers of certain tendencies, have sometimes desired to legislate standards inspired, they believe, by their interpretation of Scripture.

Over the years, the church has generally rejected these two tendencies: one leaning toward no written guidelines; the other tending toward a Pharisee-like legalism that would interpret the Bible as saying more than it says. In an attempt, however, to speak with one voice about matters that confront our members, the church offers its people a listing of subjects and related scriptures which govern conduct.

Purity of life, as we understand it, will cause a believer to wish to avoid the appearance of evil. Christians will take a strong stand against anything that pollutes or damages the body, such as intoxicating liquor, tobacco and other narcotic drugs. Medical use of drugs, such as for anesthesia for surgery, is of course not prohibited by the church.

Recognizing the attack of the devil against God's plan for the family, the Church of God defends the sacredness of the marriage relationship and abhors divorce. The church reaches out in love to those who have experienced divorce, but recommends that scriptural directives (Matthew 19-7-9, Mark 10:11, Luke 16:18) be followed by members of the church.

Daily choices in moral and ethical matters should be based on scriptural standards rather than being swayed by worldly influences, according to the church. The way men and women dress, their eating habits, their social interaction and their use of leisure time must be governed by principles of moderation, self-control and wisdom. Christians are always on display in a world that, by and large, is not under the lordship of Christ. Conversation, appearance and values will communicate to the world how seriously they take their commitment to Christ and the church.

The *Minutes* of the General Assembly contain a lengthy listing of the church's doctrinal and practical commitments with accompanying Scripture refcrences.

SUMMARY

The Church of God calls itself a New Testament church because it bases its theology on the written Word of God. Our doctrinal positions have been arrived at by careful study of the Bible, together with an understanding of historical interpretations of what it teaches.

With respect to the Christian's personal lifestyle, the church recognizes that cultures and customs change with time and distance, but God's principles are timeless and universal.

CHAPTER REVIEW

1. Why do we believe in the Trinity?
2. Explain regeneration.
3. What is the purpose of baptism in the Spirit?
4. What one evidence is universally present in the biblical instances of Spirit baptism?
5. What two ordinances besides water baptism does the Church of God observe?

Fellowship, Breaking Bread and Prayers

Suppose a man or woman says, "I want to be the ideal member of the church. Please tell me how to go about it." What should he or she be told?

A group of Church of God pastors and lay people were asked to depict the ideal church member in terms of ten descriptive phrases. When the lists were compared, sifted and finalized, with similar phrases matched, the unanimity of the description was striking. The list is reproduced here in this final chapter with commentary.

An ideal member knows what he or she believes. Just before Jesus returned to heaven, after completing His mission and establishing His church, He prayed a powerful prayer for us, recorded in John 17. As part of the prayer He said, "I pray not that thou shouldest take them out of the world, but that thou shouldest keep them from evil. They are not of the world, even as I am not of the world" (John 17:15, 16).

People have sometimes tried to conceptualize the relationship between the church and world using two circles. One manner of arranging the two circles is to place them side by side, not touching each other, like two bicycle tire rims on a garage floor. Another way of showing a relationship is by letting the circles overlap slightly, making contact at a couple of points. But the most biblical symbolism is probably a smaller circle inside a larger circle, the small one representing the church and the large one representing the world. We are *in* the world but not *of* the world.

What keeps the smaller circle intact and guards it from being absorbed into the larger one? The answer is contained in the next petition of Jesus as He continued His prayer: "Sanctify them through thy truth: thy word is truth" (John 17:17). The factor that ensures the strength, resilience and fidelity of the church, keeps it separate and maintains its identity, and prevents the world from destroying it is the truth of God—His Word.

Perhaps the single most important quality of a good church member is knowledge of the Word of God. Our beliefs are based on it; our standards are set by it; our hopes are staked on it. We must know it. If we do not know it, we can be swept away by winds of false doctrine or led into error by the whims, opinions and traditions of men.

The church provides abundant opportunities to its members for learning the Bible. Sunday school classes explore texts, sermons explain passages, study courses examine books. Beyond all the public and group activity, however, a model Christian will adopt his or her own practice of personal reading and reflection in order to know the Book.

An ideal member lives up to the truth.

The lay people and pastors who described the perfect member agreed that many people know the truth, but they are not faithful to it. The key idea in this observation is the need for consistency or dependability.

Revelation 2:13 mentions the name of Antipas, who is not mentioned elsewhere in the Bible. He is identified as a man who died as a martyr as a testimony to his faith—"Antipas . . . my faithful martyr." Antipas lies in the "Tomb of the Unknown Soldier" of Christendom solely due to his faithfulness. God evidently admired this sterling quality of the man's life so greatly that He inspired the memorialization of his name.

Consistency marks the difference between effectiveness and uselessness in Christian service. No one will respect or follow a person who is up one day, and down the next.

An ideal member seeks spiritual depth.

Two contrasting tendencies plague the church today and probably always have. One inclination is for people to enter the fellowship of believers with a mentality which says, "What are the minimum requirements? How little must I know and do to get by?" The lifestyle and testimony of such people is marginal and ineffective in satisfying their own spiritual growth needs or influencing anyone else toward God.

An opposite propensity may be for people to become emotionally experience-centered and constantly to pursue new, frenzied, power-charged sensations. Our friends in the charismatic movement have had a healthy influence on the Church of God in one sense, reminding us again that real worship ought to be fresh and spontaneous and set free of rigid forms. But if they have erred at times in certain directions, as some of their own leaders have affirmed, one of the errors is a frantic, selfish seeking after some novel experience all the time.

The ideal balance is a church member who declares himself or herself a candidate for all that God has or wants to do! This individual sincerely desires the spiritual depths of true religion. He or she cooperates with God in the reality of sanctification, continually offering up a surrendered life for God to keep cleansed and purified. He or she desires to be baptized in the Holy Spirit, consciously removing any obstacle which prevents that filling, eagerly expecting to receive from God what He has promised.

Perhaps the most obvious manifestation of the seeker after spiritual meaningfulness is a consistently maintained prayer life. Men and women of God stay in touch with Him in prayer. Two basic motivations encourage the development and maintenance of a prayer life: Jesus calls us to do it (Matthew 26:40), and prayer works.

Prayer—talking with God and listening for His voice—allows us to look beyond ourselves and focus on God. It aligns us with His purpose and His power. Where there is an absence of prayer, there is an absence of power. We are not far into the Christian life before we realize that what we do in the Lord is entirely dependent on what we are in the Lord. And what we are in the Lord wholly depends on what we receive from the Lord. The principal determinant of what we receive is the time we spend in His presence. Prayer is irreplaceable in the life of a developing child of God.

An ideal member enjoys harmony with others.

Philippians 4:2 was penned by Paul nearly two thousand years ago, but it sounds curiously up-to-date, especially when read in the Living Bible: "And now I want to plead with those two dear women, Euodias and Syntyche. Please, please, with the Lord's help, quarrel no more—be friends again."

Disharmony in the church might have done us more harm over the years than all the opposition that has come from outside. Many of us can tell stories of churches that might as well write "Ichabod" (1 Samuel 4:21) over the door because they have earned terrible reputations in the community as a result of bitter infighting.

A good member goes to great lengths to get along with everyone in the church and to build bridges between people who may have interpersonal problems.

One of the first fateful crises of the church—the event is recounted in Acts 6—had to do with groups in the church who believed that everyone was not being dealt with on a equal basis by the church leaders. God ordained that Holy Spirit-filled men of faith and prayer be appointed to solve the problem. We must recall that this was the church which was established in the shadow of the cross; these people could still hear the echo from the Upper Room. Yet, they were beset with problems that resulted from one brother or sister thinking and saying something about another. It is obvious that irreparable harm may be done when interpersonal problems in the church are not resolved.

What happens when personal problems plague a church is that the pastor's energy is exhausted in trying to deal with the situation instead of being able to attend to worthwhile spiritual tasks. People in the church choose sides and factions emerge, clearly visible to newcomers. Our Lord is the healer of divisions and is the prince of Peace; we give a lie to our testimony when we do not allow Him to work in us to handle conflict. It is another powerful testimony of grace when He is permitted to do it.

An ideal member desires a place of service.

In a bee colony, the male bees are divided into two main classes—workers and drones. The workers perform the gathering of honey, but the drones do absolutely nothing of useful service on a day-to-day basis. *Drone* has come to mean an idler, one who is good for nothing. The Lord's design for the church did not include any drones, but there are many drones present in our churches today. The model church member, on the other hand, is a person who actively seeks his or her place of ministry and service in the church.

It is crucial for us to begin where the Bible begins in the matter of Christian service. Scripture uses the imagery of the human body to illustrate the proper functioning of the church. Each member of the human body has distinct functions; in the same way, each member of the Christian church has his or her place. The usefulness with which the member serves is based on God's planning and choosing.

Most of us have observed something like this: A man or woman is selected to be Sunday school superintendent or some other officer in the church organization, only to request a short time later to be relieved of the office because of unsuitability. The individual may have been willing to serve but mismatched in the place of service. To guard against that error, God has provided for the administration of spiritual gifts in the body of Christ.

Ministry ought to be performed on the basis of spiritual giftedness.

A member sincerely interested in finding God's will for his or her life will seriously study the matter of spiritual gifts in Scripture and will be open to God's direction. Hoary traditions that restrict spiritual gifts to the apostolic age or claim that they are arbitrarily bounced around from person to person ought to be tested against the declarations of the Word of God. The Bible reveals the different gifts that God has given to the body and gives examples of their use. A faithful child of God will wish to discover, develop and employ the gift or gifts that God has given.

More basic even than the urgency of gifts is the matter of a correct spiritual disposition toward the idea of ministry and service. The ideal member will model his or her mindset against the example of Jesus. He is our great model of servant leadership. He told His followers, "I am among you as he that serveth" (Luke 22:27). He taught, "[I] . . . came not to be ministered unto, but to minister" (Matthew 20:28). Anyone who looks for a job in the church with the idea of becoming an executive who gives orders, lording authority over brothers and sisters, has not learned the spirit of the Master.

An ideal member supports the church financially.
The General Assembly has offered to local churches a covenant of membership for pastors to use when receiving new members into the fellowship of the church. It reads as follows:

> "You realize in presenting yourself for membership that you are assuming a solemn obligation, and it is expected that you will always be true to your promise and faithfully fulfill and discharge your obligation as a loyal member.

> "Do you publicly confess and testify that you know the Lord Jesus Christ as your personal Savior in the full pardon of your sins? *[The applicant will answer, I do.]*

"Are you willing to walk in the light of the Scripture as it shines upon your path? *[I am.]*

"Are you willing to abide by and subscribe to the discipline of the Church of God as outlined by the Scripture and set forth in the *Minutes of the General Assembly*? *[I am.]*

"Are you willing to support the Church with your attendance and temporal means to the best of your ability as the Lord prospers you? *[I am.]*

"Do you agree to be subject to the counsel and admonition of those who are over you in the Lord? *[I do.]*

"If there be any member who has a legal objection to any of these becoming members of the Church, the objector may now so state.

"By the authority vested in me as a minister of the Church of God, I take great pleasure in welcoming you into this membership and extending to you the right hand of fellowship. May I encourage you to call for the services of your pastor when needed.

"I have confidence that you will ever be a faithful member and a blessing to the Church and that the Church will be a blessing to you. I pray our fellowship will always be bound together with unbroken love."

Part of the blessing of church membership is the privilege and responsibility to sustain the ministry of the Church of God by involvement and support. It is a blessing that many have never discovered in practice. Consequently, many churches which could be strong are weak, and many ministries which ought to be undertaken are left undone.

Pastors are sometimes reluctant (though not all of them) to teach and preach Christian stewardship as much as they should, since they are among the obvious beneficiaries of faithful tithing and giving. Some think that preaching sermons about money makes pastors appear overly interested in their own welfare. If by some miracle of provision an endowment fund could be set up to pay all pastors so that their own interests would not seem to be in view in the minds of some of their hearers, many pastors would sense more freedom to preach the biblical plan of finance.

The Church of God has a large percentage of its membership who are tithe payers, but many others have not committed themselves to the tithe. They may bring gifts to the church but not in proportion to their income. Often the attitude toward money is a reflection of an overall view of Christian stewardship. Some believe they can give time and money and strength for everything else, then with spare time and spare money and spare strength serve the ends of God's kingdom. But the pearl of great price (Matthew 13:46) is bought only by selling small pearls; and where no pearls have been sold, obedience has not begun.

An ideal member honors the pastor.

The biblical plan for the advancement of the kingdom never envisions a spiritually elite corps of individuals who are elevated into power over a rank-and-file army of followers, creating an artificial distinction of worth or standing. Instead, the people of God are coworkers and fellow soldiers in the work of the church. God, however, has laid His hand upon certain individuals to provide leadership and direction for the local church and to give an account to Him for the members. By gifts and calling, He equips them as pastors.

Abundant scriptural evidence undergirds a call for the people of the church to honor the pastor. The instructions of Paul to a young overseer whom he had appointed is relevant to the counsel for pastors to be honored.

> Pastors who do their work well should be paid well and should be highly appreciated, especially those who work hard at both preaching and teaching. For the Scriptures say, "Never tie up the

mouth of an ox when it is treading out the grain—let him eat as he goes along!" And in another place, "Those who work deserve their pay" (1 Timothy 5:17, 18, The Living Bible).

A good member will pray for the pastor, support him financially, look for occasions to help him and build him up, increasing his effectiveness in ministry.

An ideal member recruits new members.

The biblical terminology for an individual in the context of the church family who attempts to recruit new people is *witnessc*.

A witness tells what he or she has experienced, with the aim of attracting the hearers to his or her point of view.

Christ's commission to His followers seemed to assume total involvement on the part of everyone in the witnessing aspect of the church's ministry. For example, students of the Greek text point out that the Matthew 28 account of the Great Commission contains four verbs, the literal translations of which are "going," "'make disciples," "'baptizing" and "'teaching." Only one of the four is imperative; the other three are participles. *Make disciples* is the instruction of Christ to His followers. The going, baptizing and teaching are parts of the process. The wholesale involvement is borne out in the Acts 8 record of the scattering of the believers from Jerusalem which resulted from persecution. Many Christians had to flee, although the apostles were able to remain in the city. But in many places new believers were added to the church and new churches were begun because ". . . they that were scattered abroad went every where preaching the word" (verse 4).

It is true, of course, that some individuals seem better able to present the gospel in a way that persuades and attracts new followers. The New Testament says that God sets evangelists in the church, men and women with an unusual capability of winning souls. These may be itinerant preachers who move from church to church, or they may be lay people whose witness is especially effective. The presence of evangelists in our midst, however, is not an excuse for believers not to be witnesses. The promise of the Holy Spirit is given primarily to impart power for witnessing, and this promise is ". . . unto you, and to your children, and to all that are afar off, even as many as the Lord our God shall call" (Acts 2:39). All of us are witnesses.

In the Church of God we have learned over the years that the best candidates to hear and accept our witness are our friends and the members of our families. This is true because these people know us. They know our lifestyle. They see the changes that God and the church have made in our lives. While our obligation and privilege to witness places us—as Paul said in Romans 1:14—in debt to all men, we are apt to find ourselves more effective with acquaintances than with strangers.

Recent research by the Institute for American Church Growth in Pasadena, California, has reported that the Church of God scores extremely high as being a loving, caring church. Based on studies encompassing thousands of people in 38 denominations, our church was listed second among all the churches in America as being perceived by its own people and by outsiders as a church that loves and cares for people. What a compliment!

An ideal member expects the coming of the Lord.
It is easy for Christian to become "this world' oriented. We are surrounded by worldly stimuli. We see others enjoying material things, and the natural tendency is to take our eyes off eternal values and become preoccupied with concerns of this life.

The situation is complicated when we attempt to balance the biblical counsel to provide for own households and families against the dangerous practice of storing up this world's goods.

A believer who has steeped himself or herself in the Word of God understands the temporary nature of this present world. This world order is not eternal. Heaven and earth will pass away. Keeping eternity in focus, realizing that Jesus has promised He will return and knowing His word can be trusted, an ideal Church of God member looks for and expects His soon return.

An ideal member is committed to the church.

Church is never a take-it-or-leave-it proposition as far as God is concerned. In His perspective, "Christ . . . loved the church, and gave himself for it" (Ephesians 5:25). We ought to love it with the same abandon, the same enthusiasm, the same passion.

Nothing in this book should be construed as an appeal for commitment to the church based on the idea, "If you don't come along with us and help, the church is in danger of collapse." Quite the contrary! The sacred Architect and Builder of the church said, "I will build my church and the gates of hell shall not prevail against it" (Matthew 16:18). No, individuals receive far more from the church than the church receives from individuals. A call for commitment to the church is not sounded on the basis that the church advances civilization or raises the moral climate or makes marriages happier— although all those blessings will likely be realized. The simple fact is, the church is the body of Christ. And He wants His people to be active, functioning, fulfilled members of His body.

Being a member of the Church of God will never make a man or woman a Christian, but being a Christian without being part of the church is close to meaningless.

Thank God, we have been added to the church!

CHAPTER REVIEW

1. What is perhaps the single most important quality of a good church member?
2. What marks the difference between effectiveness and uselessness in Christian service?
3. Identify the most obvious manifestation of those who seek spiritual meaningfulness.
4. How can a church member honor his or her pastor?
5. Who are the best candidates to hear and accept our witness?

Instructions and Written Review

CTC—*Added to the Church*

Instructions

1. A Certificate of Credit will be awarded when the student satisfies the requirements listed on page 13.
2. The student, at a time designated by the instructor, should prepare the written review following the guidelines listed below. The student should use blank sheets of paper and make his own outline for the review. The completed written review should be presented to the instructor for processing.
3. In the case of home study the student should present his answers to the pastor or to someone the pastor designates.

Written Review

1. Identify the nine characteristics of the ideal New Testament church.
2. What does the list of teachings of the Church of God address; what is the Declaration of Faith?
3. Explain the cyclical effect in denominational development.
4. Explain the two systems that have been combined to form the government of the Church of God.
5. What is the focal point of the denomination?
6. With what three basic categories of ministries is the church charged?
7. Differentiate between justification and sanctification.
8. Daily choices in moral and ethical matters should be based on _____ _____ and governed by principles of _____, _____ and _____.
9. What characterizes the "ideal" church member?